PENGUIN BOOKS

Stuff I've Been Reading

'Not only does it make you want to read more but, like all great books, it's also terrific company' *Metro*

'Hornby's reading recommendations are idiosyncratic and self-aware' *Sunday Times*

'Witty and shrewd . . . An utterly decent bloke with surprisingly eclectic tastes. He is as likely to be reading Orwell on Dickens as a book about comedy writing' *The Times*

'Hearteningly unpretentious . . . a hazy, entertaining journey through the book-buying and book-reading habits of an intelligent and curious reader. In many ways, Hornby is a perfect host . . . it is all carried off with self-effacing humour [by] this most charming and least snobbish of writers' *Independent*

'Books are part of life in the fullest sense here . . . he wolfs them down' *Guardian*

'Closing fast on National Treasure status . . . [Nick Hornby is] intelligent and educated without coming across as arrogant or snobbish; generally funny but sincere in all the right places' *Telegraph*

ABOUT THE AUTHOR

Nick Hornby is the author of five bestselling novels, *High Fidelity*, *About a Boy*, *How to be Good*, *A Long Way Down* and *Juliet, Naked*, as well as his most recent novel, *Funny Girl*. His non-fiction includes *Fever Pitch*, *The Complete Polysyllabic Spree* and *31 Songs*. He has also written a novel for young adults, *Slam*, as well as the screenplays for the films *Fever Pitch*, *Wild* and *An Education*, which was nominated for an Oscar. He lives in Highbury, north London.

STUFF I'VE BEEN READING

NICK HORNBY

PENGUIN BOOKS

PENGUIN BOOKS

UK | USA | Canada | Ireland | Australia
India | New Zealand | South Africa

Penguin Books is part of the Penguin Random House group of companies
whose addresses can be found at global.penguinrandomhouse.com.

Penguin
Random House
UK

First published by Viking 2013
Published in Penguin Books 2015
001

This collection copyright © Nick Hornby, 2013

The moral right of the author has been asserted

These pieces were originally published in the *Believer* magazine between August 2006
and September 2008 and between May 2010 and December 2011

Set in 11.04/13.49 pt Dante MT Std
Typeset by Jouve (UK), Milton Keynes
Printed in Great Britain by Clays Ltd, St Ives plc

A CIP catalogue record for this book is available from the British Library

A FORMAT ISBN: 978–0–241–96795–9
B FORMAT ISBN: 978–0–241–96794–2

www.greenpenguin.co.uk

MIX
Paper from
responsible sources
FSC
www.fsc.org   FSC® C018179

Penguin Random House is committed to a
sustainable future for our business, our readers
and our planet. This book is made from Forest
Stewardship Council® certified paper.

To Nick Coleman

TABLE OF CONTENTS

TABLE OF CONTENTS

TABLE OF CONTENTS

INTRODUCTION

Talking to a friend recently about the records that meant the most to me in the first twenty-one years of my life, I was struck by how many of them still mean something to me now. *Born To Run* and *Darkness On The Edge Of Town*; *Blood On The Tracks*; the first Television album; Al Green's *I'm Still In Love With You*; Patti Smith's *Horses*; *My Aim Is True* and *This Year's Model*; *Can't Buy A Thrill* and *Countdown To Ecstasy*; and dozens more . . . I can still listen to these without feeling as though I'm trying to pull back something that is best left where it is, or was. They're great albums. I don't believe that rock 'n' roll is dead, or dying, and nor am I particularly nostalgic. People are still making great albums – or great bits of albums, anyway. The mid-1970s were an astonishingly fertile period in music, however, and a lot of the records made at that time mean something to people who weren't even born when they were first released.

It doesn't work like that with books, for all sorts of reasons. Those in their late teens and early twenties about to embark upon a lifetime of serious reading very rarely read new books, for a start. Hardbacks are expensive, and we don't know what's out – only the incurably and pitiably bookish twenty-year-olds spend their weekends reading the review pages of newspapers. If we have the right friends, then they are constantly thrusting paperbacks at us and telling us to read them – now, this minute! – and these books may have been published five, ten, or even fifty years ago. And when we are young, brand-new books are useless to us as cultural capital. I could find plenty of friends who wanted to talk about the first Ramones album the week it was released in 1976, but if I had rushed out and bought John Updike's *Marry Me*, published in the same year, I'd have struggled to find a peer to impress. I don't think I had any friends who had read the *Rabbit* books, let alone anything from Updike's later oeuvre. And, most important of all, early adulthood is a time for catching up: I was at university reading English, so there was all that, but I also discovered Raymond Chandler, Kurt Vonnegut, Tom Wolfe, Hunter S. Thompson, Donald Barthelme, John Fowles and Joseph Heller.

Every so often I pick up a book that I know meant a great deal to me in those early adult years, and I'm frequently surprised by its failure to connect with my older self. Dickens, you'll be relieved to hear, still holds up pretty well. But some of the other novels that I can remember sitting up half the night to finish now seem clunky, or pretentious, or simply dull. (I had much greater tolerance for the slow and earnest back then; I would never have dared think any of these things about a published book.) I finished everything, sometimes quickly and sometimes with agonizing reluctance, and pretended to admire the things that everyone else seems to have admired. If I had been told, by a friend or a teacher or a critic or a blurb, that something was good, then I tried hard to like it. If I didn't, then I couldn't help but feel it was my fault, never the fault of the author.

I don't read like that now. I give books up, I argue with them, quite often I know better (or know myself better) than to pick certain books up in the first place. And, of course, my tastes have changed. If I had read *Marry Me* in 1976, I'd probably have found what it had to say about marriage and adult life thrilling beyond all measure, news from a land that I was travelling towards and didn't know much about. Reading it in 2011, in my early fifties, it seemed all wrong to me – dated, fearful of women, a little silly in places. Could it be that, despite literature's obsession with durability and permanence, and pop's supposed ephemerality, 1970s music is lasting better than 1970s fiction? The music has an unfair advantage: it is simple and direct, understood immediately and in its entirety, and made mostly by young people who were quite often uninterested in making sophisticated observations about the world and our place in it. Literature has to at least affect an understanding of adult life; it might be a long time before you find out that the author you loved most when you were twenty-one actually didn't know very much about anything.

So it feels as though the books I've read or reread and loved over the last ten years – the ten years in which I've been writing these columns for the *Believer* – are the books that I can stand by. Five of those years are contained in this book, and in that time I've read and written about: Muriel Spark's *A Far Cry from Kensington*; Penelope Mortimer's *The Pumpkin Eater*; David Almond's *Skellig*; Ali Smith's *The Accidental*; Charles Portis's *Norwood*; Colm Tóibín's *Brooklyn*; Patti Smith's *Just Kids*; David Kynaston's *Austerity Britain*; Carl Wilson's *Let's Talk About Love*; Mark Harris's *Pictures at a Revolution*; Sarah Bakewell's *How to Live*; James Shapiro's *1599*; Claire Tomalin's biographies of Dickens and Hardy. Reading that list back to myself now, it feels as though I'm counting off some of my favourite books, not from the last half-decade, but from my entire life as a reader. My eighteen-year-old self might not have understood why I read so much non-fiction; my thirty-year-old self would have been baffled by Penelope Mortimer's understated sardonic despair, and Carl Wilson's relativist defence of Céline Dion. But that's precisely the point: I am now the person who needs and enjoys those qualities and ideas, and this list feels like a fuller, or at least more up-to-the-minute, reflection of self than anything I could previously have managed. These loved books are me now, and previous loved books were me then, and I retain only a passing interest in the latter person.

'Why do you read such random books?' a friend asked recently.

I don't know whether he is able to plot his own reading on a straight line, or whether he's found his genre and his fields of interest and he sticks to them, but either way, I'm happy with my randomness, mostly because it never feels random to me.

Reading is a long conversation with several different people, all of them living in your head, all of them demanding your attention. There's a sports fan in my head, and a music fan. There's a needy person who is always looking for things that make him laugh, but, because he also prizes fully imagined characters and soul, frequently goes hungry. There's somebody who wants to read novels that move him. There's a father who wants to find books for his reluctant sons. There's a man who writes for a living and draws inspiration and strength from books about how other, better writers and artists did their work. There's someone who loves other people's love for books, and who is therefore a sucker for wide-eyed recommendations that begin, 'I know you'd never think about picking this book up, but trust me – it's a work of genius.' All of these people need to be addressed at periodic intervals, and when they feel they are being ignored, I find myself picking up books that I didn't know I wanted to read, presumably as a way of keeping them happy.

And the best books create yet another mouth to feed. I don't think I understood, until I read David Kynaston's magnificent, moving and insanely researched *Austerity Britain*, that I needed to know the post-war history of my country told in what seems like week-by-week detail. Now Kynaston's series – the third volume has just been published at the time of writing – has become vitally important to me: by showing me how my parents and grandparents lived, it has, like the very best fiction, taught me something about myself that I hadn't previously recognized.

I see, flicking through the 'Books Read' lists at the beginning of each column, that over the last few years I have read and loved a novel about werewolves written in blank verse, and a long narrative poem about the Mau Mau uprising, and books about the Stasi and North Korea. In each case, my interest in these subjects, hitherto unknown to me, was created and then sustained by the brilliance of the writers concerned. A couple of these books, Anna Funder's *Stasiland* and Barbara Demick's *Nothing to Envy*, were widely admired, and did quite well, but I don't know anybody else who has read Toby Barlow's terrific *Sharp Teeth* (the werewolf book) or Adam Foulds's *The Broken Word* (the Mau Mau poem); it's not that I don't like talking about books to other people who have read them, but it has long since ceased to be a motivating force.

You will probably notice that there are many omissions in both the 'Books Bought' and the 'Books Read' lists, some of them probably embarrassing, if such a feeling can ever be properly ascribed to the subject of reading. I haven't bought some big prizewinners, and I have ignored several influential and much-discussed authors. All I can say is that I haven't read them, and clearly haven't wanted to read them. This column – and the magazine in which it appears – doesn't believe in 'oughts' or 'shoulds', words which can never happily be accommodated into thoughts about culture. We believe only in reading, as much as you can, with as much goodwill as you can muster, and in a way which makes the act vitally necessary to you. This is my reading journey over the last five years, and perhaps you will find recommendations here that will complicate yours, but mostly I hope that you will recognize some of the pleasures and frustrations all book-lovers encounter. Reading journeys are still the richest, most stimulating and the cheapest journeys of all, and you don't even have to go anywhere, apart from the inside of your own head.

early Arsenal domination, our keeper Jens Lehmann was calamitously sent off for a professional foul on Barcelona's Samuel Eto'o after fifteen minutes or so. Arsenal defended heroically, despite being a man down, and then amazingly and sensationally took the lead through Sol Campbell, who's had a miserable year both on and off the pitch, what with injuries, form and the breakdown of his relationship with the designer Kelly Hoppen. Anyway, we held the lead for the best part of an hour, and then – after we'd missed good chances to go 2–0 up – fifteen minutes from the end we conceded an equalizer, followed shortly afterwards by what turned out to be Barça's winner. Like I said, this isn't the time or the place to give you a minute-by-minute account of the game. Suffice it to say that the game was more draining for me than for any of the players, none of whom have been watching Arsenal since 1968.)

Sorry. Oxford. My plan was to get myself adopted by the poet Beth Ann Fennelly and her husband, the novelist Tom Franklin. They already have a young daughter, but I can look after myself, pretty much, and I was pretty sure that I could contribute to the household income even after sending money home to my own young family. It didn't happen, in the end – something about some papers that didn't come through, unless Tom and Beth Ann were just trying to let me down gently – but I still couldn't shake the notion that their life in Mississippi was an enviable one. Maybe it would get boring after a while, drinking coffee in the sunshine on the veranda outside Square Books and walking down the road to visit Faulkner's house, but surely not for a year or two?

In an attempt to compensate for the disappointment caused by the bungling bureaucrats, my reading was exclusively Southern for a couple of weeks, and I began with Beth Ann Fennelly's collection of poems, *Tender Hooks*. I met Beth Ann and her daughter on the aforementioned veranda, admittedly only briefly (Claire will one day find it bewildering to learn that on the basis of these few minutes, I had made concerted attempts to become her extremely big brother), but both of them seemed like the kind of people that one would like to know better. And then, as luck would have it, a few days later I read 'Bite Me', the very first poem in the collection, in which Beth Ann describes her daughter's birth:

> And Lord did I push, for three more hours
> I pushed, I pushed so hard I shat,
> Pushed so hard blood vessels burst
> in my neck and in my chest, pushed so hard
> my asshole turned inside out like a rosebud . . .

So I ended up feeling as though I knew them both better anyway – indeed, I can think of one or two of my stuffier compatriots who'd argue that I now know more than I need to know. (Is now the appropriate time, incidentally, to point out the main advantage of adoption?) If I had never met mother or daughter, then these lines would have made me wince, of course, but I doubt if they would have made me blush in quite the same way; maybe one should know poets either extremely well or not at all.

Tom Franklin's novel *Hell at the Breech* – which I haven't yet read – is set in 1890s Alabama, and is by all accounts gratifyingly bloody. So from the outside it looks as though they obey old-school gender rules round at the Fennelly/Franklin place: the man writes about guns and mayhem, the lady writes about babies and home. But as the above excerpt indicates, it's not really like that at all. Yes, *Tender Hooks* is mostly about motherhood, but Fennelly's vision has more in common with Tarantino's than Martha Stewart's. One long, rich poem placed at the centre of the collection, 'Telling the Gospel Truth', puts the blood and sweat back into the Nativity, before moving on, cleverly and without contrivance, to contemplate the fatuity of poems that use 'dinner knives to check for spinach in their teeth'.

Fennelly's poems aren't mannered, needless to say. They're plain, funny and raw, and if you want to buy a present that isn't cute or dreamy for a new mother, then *Tender Hooks* will hit the spot – and won't stop hitting it even though it's sore.

Larry Brown lived in Oxford before his untimely death in 1994. *On Fire* is a terse, no-bullshit little memoir about his life as a fireman and a hunter and a father and a writer (he did all of those things simultaneously), and though I know next to nothing about the last two occupations . . . Ah, now, you see, that's precisely it. It's not true that I know next to nothing about the last two occupations, of course. I know a reasonable amount about both of them, and I was making a silly little self-deprecating joke. (There I go again. Was it silly? Was it little? Probably not. It was probably a brilliant and important self-deprecating joke.) But what struck me about Brown's memoir is that, if you have experience of firefighting and hunting, self-deprecation is inappropriate and possibly even obstructive. It's not that Brown is self-aggrandizing in any way. He isn't. But in order to describe simply and clearly how you rescued someone from a burning building, you don't want to waste words on all the throat-clearing and the oh-it-was-nothings that many of us (especially many of us in England) have to go through before we're able to say anything at all. Before I read *On Fire*, I believed that self-deprecation was a matter of taste and personality, but now I can see that it's much more a function of experience – that old joke, the one about having a lot to be modest about, is unavoidable here. There is a very precise description of the self-deprecator and his mindset in *The Sixth Heaven*, the second part of L. P. Hartley's *Eustace and Hilda* trilogy (about which more later):

> Eustace had no idea in what guise he wanted to appear to his listener – he tried to confine himself to the facts, but the facts must seem such small beer to her, with her totally different range of

experience. He tried to make them sound more impressive than they were; then he was ashamed of himself, and adopted a lighter tone, with an ironical edge to it, as if he well knew that these things were mere nothings, the faintest pattering of raindrops . . . But he thought she did not like this; once or twice she gently queried his estimate of events and pushed him back into the reality of his own feelings.

And that, of course, is the danger of self-deprecation: its avoidance of that reality. Larry Brown can confine himself to the facts, which actually aren't small beer (or certainly don't seem that way to those of us who experience no physical danger in the course of a normal working week); and as a consequence, the truth of any given situation is perhaps a lot easier to reach . . . Oh, there we are! Thank God! It was actually easier for him than it is for me! He had it cushy, with his diving into burning buildings and his, you know, his heavy equipment!

Still on my Southern kick, I read James Wilcox's gentle, rich and atmospheric *Modern Baptists*, and *True Adventures with the King of Bluegrass*, Tom Piazza's little book (it was originally a magazine article) about Jimmy Martin, in which the backstage area of the Grand Ole Opry is rather charmingly revealed to be a kind of country music limbo, where Nashville musicians wander around, apparently for ever, harmonizing and jamming with anyone they bump into. (The only bum notes are struck by Piazza's hero, who tries to pick a fight with anyone who still speaks to him.)

Baltimore isn't really in the South, I know, but when a new Anne Tyler novel is published, you have to kick whatever habit you've developed and pick it up. And then read it. *Digging to America* is, I think, my favourite of her recent books. It may be disconcerting for those of you reared on Bret Easton Ellis and Irvine Welsh to read a novel whose climactic scene deals with a parent's comical attempts to get her child to give up her pacifiers (or 'binkies', as they are known within the family); I can imagine some critics complaining that Tyler ignores 'the real world', wherever that might be – especially as Baltimore, where all her novels take place, is also the setting for *The Wire*, HBO's brilliant, violent series about drug dealers, their customers and the police officers who have to deal with them. The best answer to this actually rather unreflective carping comes from John Updike, in his *New Yorker* review of bad boy Michel Houellebecq's new novel:

> But how honest, really, is a world picture that excludes the pleasures of parenting, the comforts of communal belonging, the exercise of daily curiosity, and the widely met moral responsibility to make the best of each stage of life, including the last?

Nicely put, John. (And if there's more where that came from, maybe it's time to have a go at something longer than a book review.) Neatly, his summary of Houellebecq's omissions serves as a perfect summary of some of the themes in *Digging to America*, although the emphasis on pleasures and comforts can't do justice to Tyler's complications and confusions. Perhaps no single novel can capture the variety of our lives; perhaps even Houellebecq and Anne Tyler between them can't get the job done. Perhaps we need to read a lot.

Ali Smith's brilliant *The Accidental* manages to capture more of our lives, including both the humdrum and the uncomfortable, than any novel has any right to do. The central narrative idea (stranger walks into a family holiday home) is basic, and the book is divided into three parts: 'The Beginning', 'The Middle' and 'The End'. And yet *The Accidental* is extremely sophisticated, very wise, wonderfully idiosyncratic and occasionally very funny. (It says something about Ali Smith's comic powers that she can make you laugh

simply by listing the schedule of UK History, a British cable channel.)
Here's a little bit from the middle of the book, the section entitled
'The Middle':

> The people on the TV talk endlessly . . . They say the word middle
> a lot. Support among the middle class. No middle ground. Now to
> other news: more unrest in the Middle East. Magnus thinks about
> Amber's middle . . .

I should own up here and tell you that *The Accidental* is a literary
novel; there's no point trying to hide this fact. But it's literary not
because the author is attempting to be boring in the hope of getting
on to the shortlist of a literary prize (and here in the UK, Smith's
been on just about every shortlist there is) but because she can't figure out a different way of getting this particular job done, and the
novel's experiments, its shifting points of view and its playfulness
with language seem absolutely necessary. I can't think of a single
Believer reader who wouldn't like this book. And I know you all.

I read *The Shrimp and the Anemone*, the first part of L. P. Hartley's
Eustace and Hilda trilogy, bloody ages ago. And then I lost the book,
and then I went off on my Southern thing, and then it was way too
slow to pick up in a European Cup Final month, and . . . to get to
the point: I've now read *The Sixth Heaven*, the second part, and it
was something of a disappointment after the first. *The Shrimp and
the Anemone* is an extremely acute book about childhood because,
well, it explores the reality of the feelings involved, even though
these feelings belong to people not quite into their teens. Hartley
(who wrote *The Go-Between* and hung out in country houses with
Lady Ottoline Morrell and the like) never patronizes, and the raw-
ness, the fear and the cruelty of his young central characters chafes
against their gentility in a way that stops the novel from being inert.
In *The Sixth Heaven*, however, Eustace and Hilda are in their twenties,

and inertia has taken hold – there is a lot more hanging out in country houses with posh people than I could stomach. *The Sixth Heaven*, indeed, might have become an Unnamed Literary Novel, as per the diktats of the Polysyllabic Spree, if Hartley didn't write so wonderfully well. I nearly gave up hundreds of times, but just as I was about to do so, along came another brilliant observation. Even so, the third novel, *Eustace and Hilda*, begins with a chapter entitled 'Lady Nelly Expects a Visitor'. The first sentence reads thus: 'Lady Nelly came out from the cool, porphyry-tinted twilight of St Mark's into the strong white sunshine of the Piazza.' I fear it might be all over for me.

I have just consulted my Amazon Recommends list, just in case anything took my fancy, and the first five books were as follows:

1) *Fidgety Fish* by Ruth Galloway

2) *The Suicidal Mind* by Edwin S. Shneidman

3) *The Very Lazy Ladybird* by Isobel Finn and Jack Tickle (illustrator)

4) *Clumsy Crab* by Ruth Galloway

5) *No Time to Say Goodbye: Surviving the Suicide of a Loved One* by Carla Fine.

It will have to be *The Very Lazy Ladybird*, I think. I haven't got time for books about clumsy crabs in a World Cup month. ✶

SEPTEMBER 2006

BOOKS BOUGHT:
* *Field Notes from a Catastrophe* –
  Elizabeth Kolbert
* *The Case of Mr Crump* – Ludwig
  Lewisohn

BOOKS READ:
* None

You have probably noticed that we don't think much of scientists, here at Believer Towers. The Polysyllabic Spree, the eighty-seven white-robed and intimidatingly effete young men and women who edit this magazine, are convinced that the real work in our society is done by poets, novelists, animators, experimental film-makers, drone-metal engineers and the rest of the riff-raff who typically populate the pages of this magazine. I, however, am not so sure, which is why, after a great deal of agonized internal debate, I have decided to introduce a Scientist of the Month Award. As will become clear, this month's winner, Matthias Wittlinger of the University of Ulm, in Germany, is a worthy one, but I am very worried about several, if not all, of the months to come. I don't really know much about science, and my fear is that we'll end up giving the prize to the same old faces, month after month after month. A word in Marie Curie's ear: I hope you have plenty of room on your mantelpiece. Without giving anything away, you're going to need it.

According to the July 1 edition of the *Economist*, Matthias Wittlinger decided to investigate a long-held but never proven suspicion that what enables an ant to find his (or her) way home to the nest is an inbuilt pedometer – in other words, they count their steps. He tested this hypothesis in an ingenious way. First, he made the ants walk through a ten-metre tunnel to get food; he then made them walk back to their nests through a different ten-metre tunnel. But the fun really started once they'd got the hang of this. Wittlinger trimmed the legs of one group of ants, in order to shorten the stride pattern; another group was put on stilts made out of pig bristle, so that their steps became much bigger. The results were satisfying. The ants with little legs stopped about four metres short of the nest; the ants on stilts, meanwhile, overshot by fifteen feet. Anyone who thinks that someone other than Wittlinger is a more deserving recipient of the inaugural *Stuff I've Been Reading* Scientist of the Month Award is, to put it bluntly, an idiot. Science doesn't get any better than this.

I'm delighted for Matthias, of course, but I am also feeling a little rueful. For many years now, I've been trimming and lengthening ants' legs, mostly because the concentration and discipline involved has allowed me to forgo all sexual activity. (I have been using pieces of old guitar string for the stilts, and guitar string is funnier than pig bristle, because the ants kind of bounce along.) I wasn't, however, doing it in a particularly purposeful way – I had no idea that I could have been written about in the *Economist*, or that I could win prestigious awards. And anyway, I was making an elementary error: I was trimming and lengthening the legs of the same ants – and this, I see now, was completely and utterly pointless: three hours of microsurgery on each ant and they all ended up the same height, anyway.

Cynics don't read the *Believer*, which is fortunate, because a cynic might say that the introduction of the Scientist of the Month Award is a desperate attempt to draw attention away from the stark, sad entry under 'Books Read' at the top of this page. And a clever cynic might wonder whether the absence of read books, and therefore the appearance of the award, has anything to do with the arrival of the World Cup, a football tournament that every four years consumes the inhabitants of every country in the world bar the USA. The truth is that the World Cup allowed me to introduce the award. I'd been meaning to do it for years, but space had always prevented me from doing so. Now that I have no books to write about, I can fulfil what can be described, without exaggeration, as a lifelong dream.

I wish I had read some books this month, to be honest, and not just because I wouldn't have to drivel on about nothing for a couple of pages. It's not that I believe reading is more important than sport, but there have been moments during this last month when I knew, beyond any shadow of a doubt, that I was wasting my time and yet made no effort to turn off the TV and do something more constructive. Watching Ukraine v. Tunisia can in part be explained by my bet on Andriy Shevchenko to score during the game. (He did, after taking a dive to win a penalty that he himself took.) But I have no way of rationalizing my willingness to stick with Ukraine v. Switzerland, even after it was clear that it was going to be perhaps the most pointless and boring ninety minutes in the history of not only soccer but of all human activity. Couldn't I have read something at some point during the second half? A couple of Dylan Thomas's letters, say? They were right there, on the bookshelf behind the sofa.

It wasn't a very good World Cup. The star players all underperformed; everybody was too scared of losing; there were too few goals, too many red and yellow cards; and there was way too much cheating and diving and shirtpulling. And yet the rhythm of a World Cup day is unimprovable, if you don't have a proper job. You wake up in the morning, do a little online betting, read the previews of the games in the newspaper, maybe watch the highlights programme you recorded the previous night. The first game is at two, so just beforehand you are joined by other friends without proper jobs (some of whom won't leave until eleven that night); it finishes at four, when you repair to the garden, smoke, drink tea and kick a ball about with any of your children who happen to be there. The second game finishes at seven, just in time for bed, bath and story time, and I don't know about you, but we used the 'live pause' feature on our digital system for the eight o'clock game – there was a heat wave in Europe, and my kids took a while to get to sleep. Food was ordered at half-time and delivered during the second half. Has there ever been a better way to live than this? Friends, football, take-aways, no work . . . One can only presume that if Robert Owen and those guys had waited a couple of hundred years for the invention of the World Cup, takeaway food, digital TV and work-shy friends, there was no way any utopian experiment could have failed.

For maybe the first time in my life, however, I have begun to sympathize with Americans who find the game baffling and slow. The lack of goals has never bothered any football fan, but when it becomes clear that a team doesn't even want to score one, that they'd rather take their chances in a penalty shoot-out, then the lack of action ceases to become a matter of taste and starts to look like a fatal flaw in the tournament. If you're so scared of losing, don't enter! Stay home! Let Belgium and Lithuania play instead! Many teams played with one striker, playing all on his own against two or three defenders; England's striker Wayne Rooney became so frustrated by these odds that he attempted to even them out by stamping on the balls of one of the defenders looking after him.

We can be pretty sure that it hurts, having your testicles stamped on, but I understand that Americans have come to refer contemptuously to the more theatrical World Cup injuries as the 'flop and bawl' – the implication being, I think, that these players are feigning their distress. First of all, you must understand that the rest of the world is more susceptible to pain than you. Our smoking, our poor diets and our heightened sensitivities (to both literature and life) mean that even a slight push in the back can send excruciating agony coursing through our bodies. You, however, because of your all-meat diet and your status as a bullying superpower, feel nothing, either emotionally or physically, at any time. So you can sneer at our floppers and bawlers if you want, but what does that say about you? How can you ever understand a novel, if you don't understand pain?

And secondly, these players are terrible, awful cheats. It wasn't always like this. But ten or so years ago, those in charge of the game decided, laudably, that they wanted to encourage the more creative players, which meant penalizing the defenders whose job it was to stifle that creativity. Nobody foresaw what would happen as a result: that these creative players would spend more time trying to land their opponents with a yellow or red card than they would trying to score a goal. (A yellow card means that the recipient is frightened of making a tackle for the rest of the game; a red card means he can't take any further part. Either is useful for the opposing team, which means there's too much of an incentive to fake an injury at the moment.) In my book *Fever Pitch*, which was first published in 1992 (and you can take great literature out of the month, but you can't take it out of the man), I wrote that 'for a match to be really, truly memorable . . . you require as many of the following features as possible', and the sixth requirement listed was for a member of the opposition to receive a red card. At that time, I'd maybe seen half a dozen sendings-off in my twenty-five-year life as a fan; in the last five years, I've probably seen five times that many. It's no fun any more, and it kills the game. I withdraw my earlier ruling.

The saddest moment for me in this World Cup was watching Thierry Henry, my role model and hero and the man that both my wife and I wish had fathered our children, clutching his face after receiving a blow on the chest. *Et tu, Thierry?* Anyway, flopping and bawling now occupies the same position in our sporting culture as steroids do in yours. Crying like a baby is obviously less harmful

OCTOBER 2006

BOOKS BOUGHT:
* ✷ *Winter's Bone* – Daniel Woodrell
* ✷ *Will This Do?* – Auberon Waugh
* ✷ *Because I Was Flesh* – Edward Dahlberg
* ✷ *Clear Water* – Will Ashon
* ✷ *My Life with the Hustler* – Jamie Griggs Tevis

BOOKS READ:
* ✷ *Field Notes from a Catastrophe* – Elizabeth Kolbert
* ✷ *Imperium* – Robert Harris
* ✷ *Jimi Hendrix Turns Eighty* – Tim Sandlin
* ✷ *The Zero* – Jess Walter
* ✷ *Fun Home* – Alison Bechdel

'What we need,' one of those scary critics who write for the serious magazines said recently, 'is more straight talking about bad books.' Well, of course we do. It's hard to think of anything we need more, in fact. Because then, surely, people would stop reading bad books, and writers would stop writing them, and the only books that anyone read or wrote would be the ones that the scary critics in the serious magazines liked, and the world would be a happier place, unless you happen to enjoy reading the books that the scary critics don't like – in which case the world would be an unhappier place for you. Tough.

Weirdly, the scary critic was attempting to review a book she did like at the time, so you might have thought that she could have forgotten about bad books for a moment; these people, however, are so cross about everything that they can't ever forget about bad books, even when they're supposed to be thinking about good ones. They believe that if you stop thinking about bad books even for one second, they'll take over your house, like cockroaches. She got distracted mid-review by the *Believer* and its decision – which was taken over three years ago – to try to play nice when talking about the arts; some people are beginning to come to terms with it now, not least because they can see that very few pages of the magazine are given over to reviews. (Do we have to do the straight talking even if we're interviewing someone? Wouldn't that be rude? And pointless, given that presumably we'd be interviewing someone whose work we didn't like?)

The scary woman is not a big fan of this column, which is sad, of course, but hardly a surprise. What's more disappointing to me is that she and I go way back, right to the time when we used to bump into each other on the North of England stand-up comedy circuit, and now we seem to have fallen out. People in Bootle still talk about her impression of the Fonz. Why did she want to throw all that merriment away and become a literary editor? To borrow an old line from the late, great Tommy Cooper: 'We used to laugh when she said she wanted to be a comedian. We're not laughing now.'

I am unable, unfortunately, to do any straight talking about the books I've been reading, because they were all great. The one I enjoyed the least was Elizabeth Kolbert's *Field Notes from a Catastrophe*, and that's because she makes a very convincing argument that our planet will soon be uninhabitable. Usually, devastatingly depressing non-fiction gives you some kind of get-out: it couldn't happen here, it won't happen to me, it won't happen again. But this one really doesn't allow for much of that. Kolbert travels to Alaskan villages with permafrost experts to see how the permafrost is melting. (Hey, W. It's called permafrost. It's melting. Tell us again why there's nothing to worry about.) She visits Greenland with NASA scientists to watch the ice sheets disintegrating, listens to biologists describe how English butterflies are moving their natural habitats northwards, goes to Holland to look at the amphibious houses

STUFF I'VE BEEN READING

being built in preparation for the coming deluge. You couldn't wish for a cleaner or more concise explanation of the science – Kolbert's research is woven into her text like clues in the scariest thriller you'll ever read. There is no real debate about any of this in the scientific community, by the way. Oil companies and other interested parties occasionally try to start a debate by making claims that are clearly and criminally fallacious, on the grounds that we might believe there's an element of doubt, or that the truth lies somewhere in between, but really there's nothing to argue about. Climate change is happening now, and it will be devastating, unless unimaginably enormous steps are taken by everyone, immediately.

There is, I need hardly tell you, very little evidence that anyone in any position of authority in the USA is prepared to do what is desperately needed. Senator James Inhofe, the chairman of the Senate Committee on Environment and Public Works, believes that global warming is 'the greatest hoax ever perpetrated on the American people'; White House official Philip Cooney 'repeatedly edited government reports on climate change in order to make their findings seem less alarming' before quitting his job and going off to work for ExxonMobil.

I don't often have the urge to interview authors of non-fiction, because the book should, and invariably does, answer any questions I might have had on the subject. But I noticed in the author bio on the dust jacket that Elizabeth Kolbert, like me, has three sons. Has she talked to them about this stuff? How does it affect her morale, her ability to provide the kind of positivity and sense of security that children need? The evidence suggests that our children will be living very different, and much less comfortable, lives than our own; they may well decide that there's not much point in having children themselves. You may not want to read a book as lowering as this one, but maybe that's one of the problems anyway, that we don't want to know. If you don't want to know, then you need to take

23

your head out of your ass and read *Field Notes from a Catastrophe*. It's short, and it's rational and calm, and it's terrifying.

I picked up a manuscript of Tim Sandlin's novel *Jimi Hendrix Turns Eighty* just at the right time: not only is it funny, but it imagines a future, because that's where it's set. Sandlin's characters all live or work in Mission Pescadero, a retirement community in California, in the year 2023; almost all the old folk are pot-smoking, sexually incontinent hippies who have been sleeping with each other and arguing with each other (quite often about the original line-up of Blue Cheer) for decades. The in-house band that plays covers at the Friday night sock hop is called Acid Reflux, which may well be the most perfect fictional band name I've ever come across.

The residents of Mission Pescadero, sick of being tranquillized and denied privileges by the authoritarian staff, stage a revolution and seize control, but *Jimi Hendrix Turns Eighty* is not the sort of satire that loses its soul in an attempt to crank up the pace, and nor does it waste its characters while wrapping up its narrative. And, of course, it would have been unreadable if it had attempted to patronize or poke fun at the old, or the ageing process, but it never does that. Sandlin can see that there is a kind of gruesome comedy in what happens to us, but the humour is never mean, and he loves his people too much not to understand that their grief and nostalgia and frustration are real. This clever novel slipped down easily, and provided real refreshment in this vicious, stupefying (and, Elizabeth Kolbert has taught me, probably sinister) London summer.

Imperium is the first novel in my brother-in-law's projected trilogy about Cicero. I wrote about his last novel, *Pompeii*, in this column, and was positive that I'd have been sacked by the time his next one came out, but here we are. I won't say too much about it, other than that I have the cleverest brother-in-law a man could wish for, and that having a clever brother-in-law is enormously and gratifyingly educative. He doesn't need any help from me, anyway.

OK, I will say this: Robert's Cicero is a proper, living, breathing politician, and therefore perhaps the best fictional portrayal of the breed I've come across. Usually, the narrative in novels about politics goes like this: earnest, committed and naive young politician is made older and more cynical by the real world. Anyone who was ever at school or college with a politician, however, knows that this narrative only works as metaphor, because people who want to be politicians are never naive. Those little bastards are sneaky and ambitious even when attempting to be elected as entertainments secretary. (We need our representatives in our respective parliaments, of course we do, but they are the least representative people you could ever come across.) Robert understands this, although he's a former political reporter, so he likes politicians more than I do, and as a result, Cicero is properly complicated: attractive, devious, passionate, ferociously energetic, pragmatic. This, surely, is how he was, and I suspect our own Prime Minister must have been very similar. Your President, however, is sui generis.

I've been waiting to see how Jess Walter followed up last year's brilliant *Citizen Vince*, although I wish I'd had to wait a little longer – not because I thought his new book needed the extra time and care, but because he's not playing the game. Yes, it's perfectly possible to write a book every year – all you need to do is write 500 words a day (less than a quarter of the length of this column) for about eight months. This, however, would only leave four months of the year for holidays, watching the World Cup, messing about on the internet, judging book prizes in exotic locales, and so on. So most authors keep to a much more leisurely schedule of a book every two or three years, while at the same time managing to give the impression to publishers that books are somehow bubbling away inside them, and that any attempt to force the pace of the bubbling process would be disastrous. It's a system that works well, provided that people like Walter don't work too hard. If the various writers' unions had any real teeth, he'd be getting a knock on the door in the middle of the night.

It doesn't help that *The Zero* is a dazzlingly ambitious novel, a sort of *Manchurian Candidate*-style satire of post-9/11 paranoia. Brian Remy is a policeman involved in the clear-up of an enormous structure that has been destroyed in some sort of horrific terrorist attack. To his bewilderment, he's taken off this job and put to work on an undercover counter-terrorist organization, a job he never fully understands – partly because the task itself is dizzyingly incomprehensible, and partly because Remy suffers from blackouts, or slippages out of consciousness, which means that he wakes up in the middle of scenes with no real awareness of how he got there, or what he's supposed to be doing.

This condition is a gift, for both writer and reader – we're as compelled and as thrillingly disoriented as he is – but where Walter really scores is in the marriage of form and content. Has there ever been a more confusing time in our recent history? You didn't have to be Brian Remy to feel that life immediately post 9/11 seemed to consist of discrete moments that refused to cohere into an unbroken narrative. And there were (and are still) pretty rich pickings for paranoiacs, too. Remy keeps stumbling into huge aircraft hangars filled with people poring over bits of charred paper, and one recognizes both the otherworldliness and plausibility of these scenes simultaneously. A couple of books ago, Walter was writing (very good) genre thrillers; now there's no telling where he's going to end up. I don't intend to miss a single step of his journey.

Last month I read nothing much at all, because of the World Cup, and this month I read a ton of stuff. I am usually able to convince myself that televised sport can provide everything literature offers and more, but my faith in my theory has been shaken a little by this control experiment. Who in the World Cup was offering the sophisticated, acutely observed analysis of the parent–child relationship to be found in Alison Bechdel's extraordinary graphic novel *Fun Home*, for example? You could make an argument for Ghana, I suppose, in the earlier rounds, or Italy in the knockout stages. But let's face it, your argument would be gibberish, and whoever you were arguing with would laugh at you.

Fun Home has had an enormous amount of praise ladled on it already, and those of us who love graphic novels will regret slightly the overt literariness of Bechdel's lovely book (there are riffs on Wilde, and *The Portrait of a Lady* and Joyce) – not because it's unenjoyable or pretentious or unjustified, but because it is likely to encourage those who were previously dismissive of the form to decide that it is, after all, capable of intelligence. Never mind. We'll ignore them. *Fun Home* is still as good as the very best graphic novels, although it's a graphic memoir, rather than a novel, and as such can stand comparison with *The Liars' Club* or *This Boy's Life* or any of the best ones. Bechdel grew up in a fun(eral) home, and had a father who struggled with his homosexuality throughout his life. Despite these singularities, she has written (and drawn) a book whose truth is instantly recognizable to anyone who's ever had a complication in their youth or young adulthood. It's rich, and detailed, and clever even without the literary references.

Fun Home is, I think, a great book, yet someone, somewhere, won't like it, and will say so somewhere. If you want to do some 'straight talking', do it about the environment, or choose some other subject where there's a demonstrable truth; Elizabeth Kolbert knows that there's enough hot air as it is. ✶

APRIL 2007

One thing I knew for sure before I started Claire Tomalin's biography of Thomas Hardy: I wouldn't be going back to the work. Hardy's prose is best consumed when you're young, and your endless craving for misery is left unsatisfied by a diet of The Smiths and incessant parental misunderstanding. When I was seventeen, the scene in *Jude the Obscure* where Jude's children hang themselves 'becos they are meny' provided much-needed confirmation that adult life was going to be thrillingly, unimaginably, deliciously awful.

Now I have too meny children myself, however, the appeal seems to have gone. I'm glad I have read Hardy's novels, and equally glad that I can go through the rest of my life without having to deal with his particular and peculiar gloom ever again.

I suppose there may be one or two people who pick up Tomalin's biography hoping to learn that the author of *Tess of the D'Urbervilles* and *Jude* turned into a cheerful sort of a chap once he'd put away his laptop for the night; these hopes, however, are dashed against the convincing evidence to the contrary. When Hardy's friend Henry Rider Haggard lost his ten-year-old son, Hardy wrote to console him thus: 'I think the death of a child is never really to be regretted, when one reflects on what he has escaped.' Every cloud, and all that . . . Those wise words could only have failed to help Haggard if he was completely mired in self-pity.

Hardy died in 1928, and one of the unexpected treats of Tomalin's biography is her depiction of this quintessentially rural Victorian writer living a metropolitan twentieth-century life. It's hard to believe that Hardy went to the cinema to see a film adaptation of one of his own novels, but he did; hard to believe, too, that he attended the wedding of Harold Macmillan, who was Britain's Prime Minister in the year that the Beatles' first album was released. What happened to Hardy after his death seemed weirdly appropriate: in a gruesome attempt to appease both those who wanted the old boy to stay in Wessex and those who wanted a flashy public funeral in London, Hardy was buried twice. His heart was cut out and buried in the churchyard at Stinsford, where he'd always hoped he'd be laid to rest; what was left of him was cremated and placed in Westminster Abbey, where his pallbearers included Prime Minister Stanley Baldwin, A. E. Housman, Rudyard Kipling, George Bernard Shaw, J. M. Barrie and Edmund Gosse. Hardy was a modern celebrity, but his characters inhabited a brutal, strange, pre-industrial England.

Such is Tomalin's skill as a literary critic – and this is a book that restores your faith in literary criticism – that I did end up going back to the work, although it was the poetry, not the novels, that I read. The poems written immediately after the death of Hardy's first wife, Emma, are, as Tomalin points out, quite brilliant in their . . .

I think they've gone now. They never read on after the first couple of paragraphs, and I know they will approve of the Tomalin book, so I'm pretty sure they will leave me alone for a while, and I can tell you what's been going on here. Older readers of this magazine may recall that I had a regular column here, up until the autumn of 2006; you may have noticed that when I was removed, I was described as being 'on sabbatical' or 'on holiday', a euphemism, I can now reveal, for 'being re-educated', which is itself a euphemism – and here the euphemisms must stop – for 'being brainwashed'.

The Polysyllabic Spree, the 365 beautiful, vacant, scary young men and women who edit this magazine, have never really approved of me reading for fun, so after several warnings I was taken by force to the holding cells in the basement of their headquarters in the Appalachian Mountains and force-fed proper literature. It's a horrific place, as you can imagine; everywhere you can hear the screams of people who don't want to read *Gravity's Rainbow* very much because it's too long and too hard, or people who would rather watch *Elf* than that Godard film where people sit in wheelbarrows and read revolutionary poetry out loud. (I saw poor Amy Sedaris down there, by the way. I won't go into what they've actually done to her. Suffice to say that she won't be making any jokes for a while.)

Luckily, I have seen lots of films where 'mad' people (i.e. people whose refusal to conform results in them being labelled insane) resist all attempts by The Man to break them, and I have picked up a few tips. For example: I hid under my tongue all the Slovenian experimental novels without vowels they were trying to make me read, and spat them out later. I had a little cache of them hidden beneath my mattress, so if the worst came to the worst I could read them all at once and kill myself. Anyway, if you see me recommend a book that sounds incomprehensible, you'll know they are taking an interest in my activities again.

I have bought a lot of books and read a lot of books in the last few months, so this first post-brainwashing column is more in the nature of a representative selection than an actual diary. And, in any case, I have been told that there are certain books I have read recently, all novels, that I'm not allowed to talk about here. One beautiful, brilliant novel in particular, a novel that took me bloody ages to read but which repaid my effort many times over, was deemed unacceptable because its author apparently impregnated an important member of the Spree a while back (and some Spree members are more equal than others, obviously), and the Spree regard sex as being obstructive to the consumption of literature. What is the . . . What is the point of having a books column like this if you have to lie about what you've read?

In my tireless and entirely laudable attempts to teach myself more about the past, I have been working methodically through books about individual years, namely James Shapiro's *1599: A Year in the Life of William Shakespeare* and Jonathan Mahler's *Ladies and Gentlemen, the Bronx Is Burning: 1977, Baseball, Politics, and the Battle for the Soul of a City*. And I read the actual books, too, not just the titles and subtitles. If I read two of these year-books a week, then I'm covering a century every year, and a millennium every decade. And how many millennia are worth bothering with, really? I'm pretty excited about this project. By 2017, I should know everything there is to know about everything.

Pedants might argue that there was more to 1599 than Shakespeare, and more to 1977 than Reggie Jackson signing for the Yankees, an event that provides the spine for Jonathan Mahler's book. But this, surely, shows a fundamental lack of faith in the writer. Mahler has had a good look at 1977, and decided it was about Reggie Jackson; if he'd thought there was anything going on in the rest of the world worth writing about, then he would have chosen something else instead.

Ladies and Gentlemen, the Bronx Is Burning is not just about Reggie Jackson, of course. That New York summer there was the blackout that resulted, almost instantaneously, in twelve hours of looting and burning over an area of thirty blocks; there was a colourful mayoral race between Bella Abzug, Abe Beame, Mario Cuomo and Ed Koch; there was the Son of Sam, and Studio 54, and a World Series for the Yankees. In those few months, New York seemed to contain so much that you can believe, while reading this book, that while Mahler can't cover our planet, he has certainly touched on most of our major themes.

That phrase 'the city itself emerges as the book's major character', or variants thereof, is usually the last desperate refuge of the critical scoundrel, but Mahler pretty much pulls off the trick of anthropomorphizing New York, and the face that emerges is almost unrecognizable; certainly there's been some major plastic surgery since the 1970s, and not all of us find the stretched skin and the absence of worry lines in SoHo and the Village attractive. There's no doubt that New York is safer, less broke and more functional than it was back then. But it's impossible to read about the city that *Ladies and Gentlemen, the Bronx Is Burning* portrays so thrillingly without a little ache for something funkier.

You know I said that you should view with suspicion any book I'm recommending that sounds dull? Well, James Shapiro's *1599* isn't one of them, honestly. It's a brilliant book, riveting, illuminating and original (by which I mean, of course, that I haven't read much like it, in all my years of devouring Shakespeare biographies), full of stuff with which you want to amaze, enlighten and educate your friends. 1599 was the year Shakespeare polished off *Henry V*, wrote

As You Like It and drafted *Hamlet*. (I was partly attracted to Shapiro's book because I'd had a similarly productive 2006 – although, unlike Shakespeare, I'm more interested in quality than quantity, possibly because I've got one eye on posterity.) Shapiro places these plays in their context while trying to piece together, from all available sources, Shakespeare's movements, anxieties and interests. Both *Julius Caesar* and *Henry V* are shown to be more about England's conflict with Ireland than we had any hope of understanding without Shapiro's expert illumination; the section on *Hamlet* contains a long, lucid and unfussy explanation of how Montaigne and his essays resulted in Hamlet's soliloquies. I'd say that 1599 has to be the first port of call now for anyone teaching or studying any of these four plays, but if you're doing neither of those things, it doesn't matter. The only thing you have to care about to love this book is how and why things get written.

The 'why' is relatively straightforward: Shakespeare wrote for money. He had a wife, a new theatre and a large theatre company to support, and there was a frightening amount of competition from other companies. The 'how' is more elusive, although Shapiro does such a wonderful job of accumulating sources and inspirations that you don't really notice the absence of the man himself, who remains something of a mystery.

Claire Tomalin and James Shapiro take different paths to their writers: there is scholarship in Tomalin's book, of course, but she is more interested in the psychology of her subject, and in exercising her acute, sensitive critical skills than she is in history. Both books, though, are exemplary in their ability to deepen one's understanding for and appreciation of the work, in their delight in being able to point out what's going on in the lines on the page. We're lucky to have both of these writers at the top of their game in the here and now.

Robert Altman's *Nashville* is one of my favourite films – or, at least, I think it is. I haven't seen it in a while, and the last time I did,

I noticed the longueurs more than I ever had before. Maybe the best thing to do with favourite films and books is to leave them be: to achieve such an exalted position means that they entered your life at exactly the right time, in precisely the right place, and those conditions can never be recreated. Sometimes we want to revisit them in order to check whether they were really as good as we remember them being, but this has to be a suspect impulse, because what it presupposes is that we have more reason to trust our critical judgements as we get older, whereas I am beginning to believe that the reverse is true. I was eighteen when I saw *Nashville* for the first time, and I was electrified by its shifts in tone, its sudden bursts of feeling and meaning, its ambition, its occasional obscurity, even its pretensions. I don't think I'd ever seen an art movie before, and I certainly hadn't seen an art movie set in a world I recognized. So I came out of the cinema that night a slightly changed person, suddenly aware that there was a different way of doing things. None of that is going to happen again, but so what? And why mess with a good thing? Favourites should be left where they belong, buried somewhere deep in a past self.

Jan Stuart's *The Nashville Chronicles* is a loving account of the making of the film, and reading it was a good way of engaging with Altman's finest seven hours, or however long the thing was, without having to wreck it by watching it for a fourth or fifth time. And, in any case, Nashville is a film that relies on something other than script (which was thrown out of the window before shooting started) and conventional methods of film-making for its effects, so a book like this is especially valuable in helping us understand them. There was Altman's apparently haphazard casting – one actor was chosen when he came to another's house to give him guitar lessons, and Shelley Duvall was a student research-scientist before being co-opted into Altman's regular troupe. There was his famous vérité sound, which required the invention of a new recording system,

MAY 2007

I have been listening to my iPod on 'shuffle' recently and, like everyone else who does this, I became convinced that my machine was exercising a will of its own. Why did it seem to play Big Star every third song? (All iPod users come to believe that their inanimate MP3 players have recondite but real musical tastes.) And how come, if you shuffle for long enough, the initial letters of the artists picked spell out the names of your children? Confused, as always, by this and most other matters, I remembered that an English magazine had extracted a book about the iPod in which the author had dealt with the very subject of the non-random shuffle. The book turned out to be Steven Levy's *The Perfect Thing*, a cute (of course) little (naturally) white (what else?) hardback history of the iPod – or at least, that is how it's billed. (The British subtitle of the book is 'How the iPod Became the Defining Object of the Twenty-First

Century'.) What the book is actually about, however – and maybe most books are, these days – is my predilection for 1980s synth-pop.

I am not speaking metaphorically here. In an early chapter of the book, Mr Levy describes, for reasons too complicated to explain, how a fellow writer was caught listening to 'a pathetic Pet Shop Boys tune, the sort of thing Nick Hornby would listen to on a bad day'. Now, I'm almost certain that this is supposed to be me, even though I don't recognize my own supposed musical tastes. (The Pet Shop Boys are a bit too groovy for my liking, and their songs don't have enough guitar on them.) I am relieved to hear, however, that I have good days and bad days, which at least opens up the possibility that on a good day I might be listening to something a little more au courant – Nirvana, say, or early Britney Spears.

Aren't people rude? It's something I don't think one can ever get used to, if you live a semi-public life – and writers, by definition, can never go any more than semi-public, because not enough people are interested in what we do. It doesn't happen often – I don't seem to have cropped up in Orwell's essays, for example – but when it does, it's always a shock, seeing yourself in a book, listening to music you don't listen to (not, as Jerry Seinfeld said, that there's anything wrong with the Pet Shop Boys), put there by someone you have never met and who, therefore, knows nothing about you . . . And what has the band done to deserve this, to borrow one of their song titles? They were mentioned in my newspaper this morning, in a diary piece about their plans for a musical adaptation of Francis Wheen's brilliant biography of Marx; that, like so much they have done, sounds pretty cool to me. Unnerved, I skipped straight to his chapter about whether the shuffle feature is indeed random. It is, apparently.

The annoying thing about reading is that you can never get the job done. The other day I was in a bookstore flicking through a book called something like *1001 Books You Must Read Before You Die* (and, without naming names, you should be aware that the task set by the title is by definition impossible, because at least 400 of the books suggested would kill you anyway), but reading begets reading – that's sort of the point of it, surely? – and anybody who never deviates from a set list of books is intellectually dead, anyway. Look at the trouble Orwell's essays got me into. First of all there's his long and interesting consideration of Henry Miller's *Tropic of Cancer*, a novel that I must confess I had written off as dated smut; George has persuaded me otherwise, so I bought it. And then, while discussing the Orwell essays with a friend, I was introduced to Norman Lewis's astounding *Naples '44*, a book which, my venerable friend seemed to be suggesting, was at least a match for any of Orwell's non-fiction. (Oh, why be coy? My venerable friend was Stephen Frears, still best known, I like to think, as the director of *High Fidelity*, and an endless source of good book recommendations.)

I think he's right. The trouble with the Orwell essays is that they are mostly of no earthly use to anyone now – and this is perhaps the first book I've read since I started this column that I can't imagine any American of my acquaintance ploughing through. If you really feel you need to read several thousand words about English boys' weeklies of the 1930s, then I wouldn't try to stop you, but these pieces are mostly top-drawer journalism – Tom Wolfe, as it were – rather than Montaigne; Orwell is dissecting bodies that actually gave up the ghost eighty-odd years ago. This problem becomes particularly acute when he's dissecting bodies that gave up the ghost ninety or a hundred years ago:

> In 1920, when I was about seventeen, I probably knew the whole of [A. E. Housman's] *A Shropshire Lad* by heart. I wonder how much impression *A Shropshire Lad* makes at this moment on a boy of the same age and more or less the same cast of mind? No doubt he has heard of it and even glanced into it; it might strike him as rather cheaply clever – probably that would be about all.

If you try to do Orwell the service of treating him as a contemporary writer, someone whose observations make as much sense to us now as they did in 1940, then that last sentence is merely hilarious – how many bright seventeen-year-old boys do you know who might have glanced into *A Shropshire Lad* and found it 'cheaply clever'? So even when Orwell is talking about things that he knows haven't lasted, he is unable to anticipate their complete and utter disappearance from the cultural landscape. How was he to know that the average seventeen-year-old boy is more likely to have sampled his sister's kidney than Housman's poetry? It wasn't his fault. He couldn't see 50 Cent coming.

An essay entitled 'Bookshop Memories', about Orwell's experiences working in a second-hand bookstore, notes that the three bestselling authors were Ethel M. Dell, Warwick Deeping and Jeffrey Farnol. 'Dell's novels, of course, are read solely by women' – well, we all knew that – 'but by women of all kinds and ages and not, as one might expect, merely by wistful spinsters and the fat wives of tobacconists.' Ah, those were the days, when popular novelists were able to rely on the fat wives of tobacconists for half their income. Times are much harder (and leaner) now. Many is the time that I've wished I could tell the size-zero wives of tobacconists that I didn't want their rotten money, but I have had to button my lip, regrettably. I have a large family to support.

One of the most bewildering lines comes in 'Inside the Whale', the long essay about the state of literature, first published in 1940, that begins with the appreciation of Henry Miller:

> To say 'I accept' in an age like our own is to say that you accept concentration-camps, rubber truncheons, Hitler, Stalin, bombs, aeroplanes, tinned food, machine-guns, putsches, purges, slogans, Bedaux belts, gas-masks, submarines, spies, provocateurs, press-censorship, secret prisons, aspirins, Hollywood films and political murders.

Is it possible to accept, say, tinned food, Hollywood films and aspirin without accepting Stalin and Hitler? I'm afraid I am one of those cowards who would have happily invaded Poland if it meant getting hold of a couple of pills to alleviate a hangover. And what was wrong with tinned food, that all those guys banged on about it so much? (Remember Sir John Betjeman's poem 'Slough'? 'Come, bombs, and blow to smithereens / Those air-conditioned, bright canteens / Tinned fruit, tinned meat, tinned milk, tinned beans / Tinned minds, tinned breath.') It's true, of course, that fresh fruit is better for you. But one would hope that, with the benefit of hindsight, Orwell, Betjeman and the rest would concede that Belsen and the purges ranked higher up the list of the mid-twentieth century's horrors than a nice can of peaches. Mind you, when in fifty years' time, students examine the intellectual journalism of the early twenty-first century, they will probably find more about the vileness of bloggers and reality television than they will about the destruction of the planet.

There are some brilliant lines. How about this, from Orwell's essay on Dickens:

> What people always demand of a popular novelist is that he shall write the same book over and over again, forgetting that a man who would write the same book twice could not even write it once.

There's a great little essay called 'Books v. Cigarettes', although some will find his conclusion (books) controversial. And, of course, his prose is beyond reproach: muscular, readable, accessible.

Naples '44, however, is something else altogether. Norman Lewis, who lived to be ninety-five and who published his last travel book in 2002, was an intelligence officer for the Allies; what he found when he was posted to Naples beggared belief. The Neapolitans were starving – they had eaten all the fish in the aquarium, and just about every weed by the roadside. An estimated 42,000 of the city's 150,000 women had turned to prostitution. And yet there is so much in this short diary other than sheer misery, so many tones and flavours. You might wish to point out that Lewis wasn't one of the starving, and so accessing flavours wasn't a problem for him, but the variety and richness and strangeness of life in what remains one of the maddest and most neurotic cities in the world clearly demanded his attention. This is a long-winded way of saying that this book is, at times, unbearably sad, but it is also very funny and weird, too. There are the doctors who specialize in the surgical restoration of virginity (although before you book your flights, ladies, you should check that they're still working), and there are the biannual liquefactions and solidifications of the blood of saints, the relative speeds of which presage either prosperity or poverty for the city. Vesuvius erupts in the middle of all this; and, of course, there's a war going on – a war which is occasionally reminiscent of the one Tobias Wolff described in *In Pharaoh's Army*. It allows for strange, pointless, occasionally idyllic trips out into the countryside, and the enemy is all around but invisible.

My favourite character, one who comes to symbolize the logic of Naples, is Lattarullo, one of the four thousand or so lawyers in Naples unable to make a living. Much of his income before the war came from acting as an 'uncle from Rome', a job which involved turning up at Neapolitan funerals and acting as a dignified and sober out-of-towner, in direct contrast to the frenzied and grief-stricken native relatives. Paying for an uncle from Rome to turn up showed a touch of class. During the war, however, Lattarullo was denied even this modest supplement because Rome was occupied, and travel was impossible. So even though everyone knew Roman uncles came from Naples, the appearance of a Roman uncle at a Neapolitan funeral before the liberation of Rome would have punctured the illusion, like a boom mic visible in a movie. This is Orwell via Lewis Carroll, and if I read a better couple of hundred pages of non-fiction this year, I'll be a happy man.

If, at the moment, you happen to be looking for a book that makes you feel good about sex, though, then I should warn you that this isn't the one. There are too many devout Catholic wives selling themselves for a tin of fruit, and way too many sexual diseases. William Kennedy's *Ironweed* is beautiful – haunted and haunting, thoughtful and visceral. But, like *Naples '44*, it is entirely without aphrodisiacal qualities. The people are too sick, and drunk, and cold, but they try it on anyway, sometimes just so they can get to sleep the night in a deserted car full of other bums. None of this matters so much to me any more. By the time you read this I will have turned fifty, so I can't reasonably expect very much more in that department, anyway. But you – you're young, some of you. I don't want you to feel bad about your bodies. Yes, you will die, and your bodies will decay and rot way before then, anyway. But you shouldn't feel bad about that just yet. Actually, on second thoughts, the truth is that *Ironweed* is exactly the sort of book you should be reading when you're young, and still robust enough to slough it off. And it's a truly terrible book to be reading in the last few months of your forties. Is this really all that's left? ★

impatient. 'A perfect day begins in death, in the semblance of death, in deep surrender,' the novelist (or his omniscient narrator) tells us. Does it? Not for me it doesn't, pal. Unless, of course, death here means 'a good night's sleep'. Or 'a strong cup of coffee'. Maybe that's it? 'Death' = 'a strong cup of coffee' and 'the semblance of death' = some kind of coffee substitute, like a Frappuccino? Then why doesn't he say so? There is no mistaking what the word 'death' means in Politkovskaya's diaries, and once again I found myself wondering whether the complication of language is in inverse proportion to the size of the subject under discussion. Politkovskaya is writing about the agonies of a nation plagued by corruption, terrorism and despotism; the highly regarded literary figure is writing about some middle-class people who are bored of their marriage. My case rests.

The highly regarded literary figure recently quoted Irwin Shaw's observation that 'the great machines of the world do not run on fidelity', in an attempt to explain his views on matrimony, and though this sounds pretty good when you first hear it, lofty and practical all at the same time, on further reflection it starts to fall apart. If we are going to judge things on their ability to power the great machines of the world, then we will have to agree that music, charity, tolerance and bacon-flavoured potato chips, to name only four things that we prize here at the *Believer*, are worse than useless.

It wasn't just the opacity of the prose that led me to abandon the novel, however; I didn't like the characters who populated it much, either. They were all languidly middle class, and they drank good wine and talked about Sartre, and I didn't want to know anything about them. This is entirely unreasonable of me, I accept that, but prejudice has to be an important part of our decision-making process when it comes to reading, otherwise we would become overwhelmed. For months I have been refusing to read a novel that a couple of friends have been urging upon me, a novel that received wonderful reviews and got nominated for prestigious prizes. I'm sure it's great, but I know it's not for me: the author is posh – posh English, which is somehow worse than posh American, even – and he writes about posh people, and I have taken the view that life is too short to spend any time worrying about the travails of the English upper classes. If you had spent the last half-century listening to the strangled vowels and the unexamined and usually very dim assumptions that frequently emerge from the mouths of a certain kind of Englishman, you'd feel entitled to a little bit of inverted snobbery.

I'm not sure, then, quite how I was persuaded to read *In My Father's House*, Miranda Seymour's memoir about her extraordinary father and his almost demented devotion to Thrumpton Hall, the stately home he came to inherit. George Seymour was a terrible snob, pathetically obsessed by the microscopic traces of blue blood that ran through his veins, comically observant of every single nonsensical English upper-class propriety – until he reached middle age, when he bought himself a motorbike and drove around England and Europe with a young man called Nick, with whom he shared a bedroom. Nick was replaced by Robbie, whom George called Tigger, after the A. A. Milne character; when Robbie shot himself in the head, a weeping George played the Disney song on a scratchy vinyl record at the funeral service. Actually, you can probably see why I was persuaded to read it: it's a terrific story, and Miranda Seymour is too good a writer not to recognize its peculiarities and its worth. Also, the same people who have been telling me to read the posh novel told me to read the posh memoir, and I felt that a further refusal would have indicated some kind of Trotskyite militancy that I really don't feel. It's more a mild distaste than a deeply entrenched world view.

Miranda Seymour owns up to having inherited her father's snobbery, which meant that I was immediately put on the alert, ready to abandon the book and condemn the author to the legions of the unnameable, but there is nothing much here to send one to the barricades. There is one strange moment, however, a couple of sentences that I read and reread in order to check that I wasn't missing the irony. When Seymour goes to visit some of her father's wartime friends to gather their recollections, she finds herself resenting what she perceives as their feelings of superiority. They saw active service and George Seymour didn't, and the daughter is defensive on the father's behalf: 'I've plenty of reason to hate my father, but his achievement matches theirs. They've no cause to be disdainful. They fought for their country; he gave his life to save a house.'

Where does one begin with this? Perhaps one should simply point out that George died in his bed (a bed within a bedroom within one of Britain's loveliest houses) at the age of seventy-one, so the expression 'he gave his life' does not have the conventional meaning here; a more exact rendering would be something like 'he put aside an awful lot of time . . .' It's a curious lapse in judgement, in an otherwise carefully nuanced book.

A couple of years ago, I wrote in this column about Michael Lewis's brilliant *Moneyball*; when I found during a recent trip to New York that Lewis had written a book about football, I was off to the till before you could say 'Jackie Robinson'. *The Blind Side* is very nearly as good, I think, which is saying something, seeing as *Moneyball* is one of the two or three best sports books I have ever read. It cleverly combines two stories, one personal, the other an account of the recent history of the game; Lewis explains how left tackle became the most remunerative position in the game, and then allows the weight of this history to settle on the shoulders of one young man, Michael Oher, currently at Ole Miss (I'm finding my effortless use of the American vernacular strangely thrilling). Oher is six feet six, weighs 330 pounds, and yet he can run hundreds of yards in fractions of seconds. He is, as he keeps being told, a freak of nature, and he is exactly what every football team in the USA is prepared to offer the earth for.

He has also had a life well beyond the realms of the ordinary, which makes his story – well, I'm afraid my knowledge of the terminology has already been exhausted, so I don't have the appropriate analogy – but in my sport we'd describe it as an open goal, and Lewis only has to tap the ball in from a couple of feet. I don't wish to diminish the author's achievement. Lewis scores with his customary brio, and the recognition of a good story is an enviable part of his talent. But who wouldn't want to read about a kid who was born to a crack-addict mother and part-raised in one of the poorest parts of one of America's poorest cities, Memphis, and ended up being adopted by a wealthy white Christian couple with their own private plane? This is material that provides the pleasures of both fiction and non-fiction. There's a compelling narrative arc, a glimpse into the lives of others, a wealth of information about and analysis of a central element of popular American culture. There's a touching central relationship, between Oher and his adoptive parents' young son, Sean Jr. There is even a cheesy, never-say-die heroine, Oher's adoptive mother, Leigh Anne Tuohy, whose extraordinary determination to look after a boy not her own is Christian in the sense too rarely associated with the American South. This would make a great movie, although you'd need a lot of CGI to convince an audience of Michael Oher's speed and size.

The Blind Side is funny, too. Michael's first game for his high school is made distinctive by him lifting up his 220-pound opponent and taking him through the opposition benches, across the cinder track surrounding the pitch, and halfway across a neighbouring field before he is stopped by players and officials from both sides. (Oher had been irritated and surprised by the opponent's trash-talking – he later told his coach he was going to put the lippy kid back on his team bus.) And the formal interview between Oher and an investigator from the NCAA, the organization whose job it is to determine whether any illegal inducements have been offered to influence a promising footballer's choice of college, is equally memorable. It's not just Oher's attempts to list his brothers and sisters that baffle the investigator; it's the opulence of his surroundings, too. The Tuohys are Ole Miss alumni, desperate for Michael to take the scholarship being offered by their alma mater, while trying to avoid putting inappropriate pressure on him. But isn't Oher's whole new life – the access to the jet, the new car, the pool, the exclusive private high school – a form of inappropriate pressure? The baffled investigator eventually decides not, but she is clearly perplexed by the atypicality of the arrangement.

Ian McEwan has hit that enviable moment that comes to a novelist only very rarely: he has written himself into a position where everyone wants to read his latest book now, today, before any other bastard comes along and ruins it. He's genuinely serious and genuinely popular, in the UK at least, and in an age where our tastes in culture are becoming ever more refined, and therefore ever more fractured, he is almost single-handedly reviving the notion of a chattering class by providing something that we can all chatter about. *On Chesil Beach* is, for me, a return to top form after the unevenness of *Saturday*. It's unusual, on occasions painfully real, and ultimately very moving.

Philip Larkin famously wrote that 'Sexual intercourse began / In nineteen sixty-three / (Which was rather late for me) / Between the end of the *Chatterley* ban / And the Beatles' first LP.' *On Chesil Beach* is set on a July night in 1962, and sexual intercourse is about to begin for Edward and Florence, married that afternoon, and painfully inexperienced. Edward wants it and Florence doesn't, and that, pretty much, is where the drama and the pain of the novel lie.

On Chesil Beach is packed with all the period detail one might expect, and occasionally it can feel as though McEwan's working off a checklist; there's the bad food, the CND marches, the naivety about the Soviet Union, the social-realist movies, the Beatles and the Stones . . . Hold on a minute. The Beatles and the Stones? 'He played her "clumsy but honourable" cover versions of Chuck Berry songs by the Beatles and the Rolling Stones.' Well, not before July 1962 he didn't. (The sentence refers to the couple's courtship.) What's strange about this anachronism is that McEwan must, at some stage, have thought of the Larkin poem when he was writing this – it might even have inspired him in some way. So if the Beatles' first LP was released in the same year sexual intercourse was invented, what exactly was he playing her in the months leading up to July 1962? 'Love Me Do' was released towards the end of that year, and there was nothing else recorded yet; the Stones, meanwhile, didn't produce anything until the following year. Does it matter? It didn't affect my enjoyment of the book, but I suspect that it does, a little. The Beatles really did belong to a different age, metaphorically and literally. I hereby offer my services as a full-time researcher.

On Chesil Beach is so short that it's actually hard to talk about without revealing more than you might want to know. You should read it, and be thankful that you grew up in a different age, where all matters sexual were a whole lot easier. Too easy, probably. Some of you younger ones are probably having sex now, absentmindedly, while reading this. You probably don't even know that you're having sex. You'll look down or up at the end of this paragraph and think, 'Eeek! Who's that?' Well, that can't be right, can it? Surely things have gone too far the other way, if that's what's happening? I'm off to read some Jane Austen. ✱

AUGUST 2007

BOOKS BOUGHT:
* *The Ha-Ha* – Jennifer Dawson
* *Poppy Shakespeare* – Clare Allan
* *Yo, Blair!* – Geoffrey Wheatcroft
* *Salmon Fishing in the Yemen* – Paul Torday
* *The Myth of the Blitz* – Angus Calder
* *This Book Will Save Your Life* – A. M. Homes

BOOKS READ:
* *Across the Great Divide: The Band and America* – Barney Hoskyns
* *Stasiland: Stories from Behind the Berlin Wall* – Anna Funder
* *Yo, Blair!* – Geoffrey Wheatcroft
* *The Ha-Ha* – Jennifer Dawson
* *Coming Through Slaughter* – Michael Ondaatje
* *Poppy Shakespeare* – Clare Allan

On the face of it, the Stasi and the Band had very little in common. Closer examination, however, reveals the East German secret police force and the brilliant genre-fusing Canadian rock group to be surprisingly . . . Oh, forget it. I don't have to do that stuff in this column – or at least, if I do, nobody has ever told me. It goes without saying that the two wires that led me to the books by Barney Hoskyns and Anna Funder came from different sockets in the soul, and power completely different, you know, electrical / spiritual devices: *Stasiland* and *Across the Great Divide* are as different as a hairdryer and a Hoover. Yes. That's it. I'm the first to admit it when my metaphors don't work, but I'm pretty sure I pulled that one off. (I wish I'd hated them both. Then I could have said that one sucks, and the other blows. Regrettably, they were pretty good.)

The journey/length of cable that led me to the Hoskyns book began a couple of years ago, when I was just about to walk out of a music club. We'd gone to see the support act, but the headliners had this amazing young guitar player called James Walbourne, an unearthly cross between James Burton, Peter Green and Richard Thompson; Walbourne's fluid, tasteful, beautiful solos drop the jaw, stop the heart and smack the gob, all at the same time. We still walked out of the club, because we really wanted a pizza, and pizza always beats art, but I was determined to track him down and make sure that I hadn't been imagining it all. I've seen him a few times since – when he's not playing with the Pernice Brothers or Son Volt or Tift Merritt, he's been appearing with his own band in a pub not far from me – and he's recently taken to playing a cover of the Band's 'Ain't No More Cane', a song off *The Basement Tapes*. So then I had a fit on the Band – I have pretty much listened to every single track on the box set that came out last year – and then I noticed that I had an unread 1993 biography on my shelves. Before long I was being taken from Stratford, Ontario, to the Mississippi Delta and on to Los Angeles.

In one crucial way, writing about the Band is difficult: Greil Marcus got there first, in his book *Mystery Train*, and Marcus's essay is still the best piece of rock criticism I have ever read. (There are thirty-seven separate index entries for Greil Marcus in *Across the Great Divide*, and yet Hoskyns still feels it necessary to get sniffy about a couple of factual errors that Marcus made in his writings. You'd have hoped that Hoskyns could have been more forgiving, seeing as how his own book would have been a lot shorter without Marcus's help.) And yet there's something irresistible about the story too, because it's the story of white rock and roll. Here's Robbie Robertson, aged sixteen, getting on a train and heading down to the American South from Canada, to play R&B covers with Ronnie Hawkins's Hawks; Robertson's pilgrimage from white Sleepytown to the birthplace of the blues was the one that millions of teenage guitarists made, in their heads at least, at the beginning of the sixties. (It may even still go on. I would imagine that James Walbourne has made exactly the same trip, and maybe not even symbolically. He lives in Muswell Hill, North London, which is sort of like Canada.) And here's Robbie Robertson, in his early thirties, bombed out of his head on cocaine, living with Martin Scorsese in a house on Mulholland Drive that had blackout covers on the windows so that the residents no longer knew or cared whether it was day or night. That, in a nutshell, is what happened to our music between the early sixties and the mid-seventies: the geographical shift, the decadence and the obliviousness to the outside world. Thank heaven for punk. And Abba.

I may be the only person in the world who has just read *Across the Great Divide* after seeing James Walbourne play 'Ain't No More Cane'. I can't imagine I'm the only person in the world who has read *Stasiland* after seeing *The Lives of Others* in my local cinema. I left that film wanting to know more about the chilling weirdness of life in the old GDR, and Anna Funder's brilliant book is full of stories that not only leave you open-mouthed at the sheer lunatic ambition of the totalitarian experiment but break your heart as well, just as they should do.

Funder reviewed *The Lives of Others* in a recent issue of *Sight & Sound*, and argued persuasively that, while it was a great film on its own terms, it bore little resemblance to life as it was lived behind the Berlin Wall: the movie was too bloodless, and there never was and never could be such a thing as an heroic Stasi officer. Her book is personal and anecdotal: she tells the stories she has come across, some of which she discovers when she places an advertisement in a local newspaper in an attempt to contact former Stasi members. This approach is perfect, because you don't need anything other than personal anecdote to tell a kind of truth about the Stasi, because they knew everybody – that was the point of them. So who wouldn't have a story to tell?

I'd be doing you and the book a disservice if I recommended it to you simply as an outstanding work of contemporary history. I'm guessing that a fair few of you are writers, and one of the unexpected strengths of this book is the implausibility of the narratives Funder unearths – narratives that nevertheless, and contrary to all perceived wisdom, seem to resonate, and illuminate, and illustrate even greater truths. Frau Paul gives birth to a desperately sick baby just as the Wall is being built; one morning she wakes up to find that it has separated her from the only hospital that can help her son. Doctors smuggle him, without her permission, over the Wall. He lives in the hospital for the next five years.

Frau Paul is given only agonizingly sporadic permission to visit her child, and she and her husband decide, perhaps not unnaturally, that they will try to escape to West Berlin. Their plans are discovered; Frau Paul refuses to cut a deal that will endanger a young man in the West who has been helping her and others. She is sent to prison. Her son is nearly five years old when he is finally allowed home. (It's interesting, incidentally, that the central characters in *The Lives of Others* are all childless. I suspect children tend to limit the range of moral choices.)

There are, it seems, stories like this on every street corner of the old East Germany, insane stories, stories that defy belief and yet unfold with a terrible logic, and Anna Funder's weary credulity, and her unerring eye for the unimaginable varieties of irony to be found in a world like this, make her the perfect narrator. Believe it or not, there are some funny bits.

It was our Prime Minister's tenth anniversary recently, and by the time you get to read this he'll be gone anyway, so it seemed appropriate to give him a little bit of consideration. Not much – Geoffrey Wheatcroft's polemic is only 120-odd pages long – but the time it took me to read it was precisely the sort of time I wanted to give him. The title refers to the President's form of address during the disastrously revealing conversation Blair had with Bush during the G8 meeting in Russia last year, when an open mic revealed the true nature of their relationship to be something closer to the one between Jeeves and Bertie Wooster than that between two world leaders, although obviously Jeeves was less servile.

Wheatcroft overstates his case a little: however much you hate Blair, it's hard to hear that his soppy Third Way contains undertones of the Third Reich. But when you see the crimes and misdemeanours piled up like this, it's hard to see how we managed to avoid foreign invaders intent on regime change. It's not just Iraq and the special relationship with the USA, although it's quite clear now that this is how Blair will be remembered. It's the sucking up to the rich and powerful (Berlusconi, Cliff Richard), the freeloading, the pathetic little lies, the broken promises, the apparent absence of any sort of conviction, beyond the conviction of his own rectitude. This book introduced me to a very handy word: 'antinomian'. (Oh, come on. Give me a break. I can't know everything. Where would I put it? And think of all the other hundreds of words I've used in this column.) You are antinomian, apparently, when your own sense of self-righteousness allows you to do anything, however mean or vicious or morally bankrupt that thing might appear to be. It's been a while, one suspects, since this word could be legitimately applied to a world leader; even Nixon and Kissinger may have slept uneasily for a couple of nights after they bombed Cambodia.

Here is the best definition of a good novel I have come across yet – indeed, I suspect that it might be the only definition of a good novel worth a damn. A good novel is one that sends you scurrying to the computer to look at pictures of prostitutes on the internet. And as Michael Ondaatje's *Coming Through Slaughter* is the only novel I have ever read that has made me do this, I can confidently assert that *Coming Through Slaughter* is, ipso facto, the best novel I have ever read.

Regrettably, the pictures in question are by E. J. Bellocq, a central character in *Coming Through Slaughter*, which means that they have a great deal of redeeming cultural import (Susan Sontag wrote a brilliant introduction to a published collection of his work); when I read a novel that allows me to ransack the internet for prostitute pictures willy-nilly, this column will be awarding a prize worth more than any genius grant.

I had been having some trouble with the whole idea of fiction, trouble that seemed in some way connected with my recent landmark birthday; it seemed to me that a lot of novels were, to be blunt, made up, and could teach me little about the world. Life suddenly seemed so short that I needed facts, and I needed them fast. I picked up *Coming Through Slaughter* in the spirit of kill or cure, and I was cured – I have only read fiction since I finished it. It's sort of ironic, then, that Ondaatje's novel ended up introducing me to an important photographer, anyway. (Oh, come on. Give me a break, I can't know everyone. Where would I put them? And think of all the other . . . No, you're right. You can only use this argument seven or eight hundred times before it begins to sound pathetic.)

Coming Through Slaughter, Ondaatje's first novel, is an extraordinary, and extraordinarily beautiful, piece of myth-making, a short, rich imagining of the life of Buddy Bolden, a New Orleans cornettist widely regarded as one of the founders of jazz. It seems to me as though anybody who has doubts about the value of fiction should read this book: it leaves you with the sort of ache that non-fiction can never provide, and provides an intensity and glow that, it seems to me, are the unique product of a singular imagination laying its gauze over the brilliant light of the world. Ondaatje writes about the music wonderfully well: you couldn't ask for anyone better to describe the sound of the crack that must happen when one form is being bent too far out of shape in an attempt to form something else. And Bolden's madness – he is supposed to have collapsed during a carnival procession – provides endless interesting corridors for Ondaatje to wander around in. I am still thinking about this novel, remembering the heat it threw off, weeks after finishing it.

I am a literal-minded and simple soul, so since then I have read nothing but novels about mentally ill people. If it worked once, I reasoned, then there's no reason why it shouldn't work every time, and I was right. I have now taken a broad enough sample, and I can reveal that nobody has ever written a bad novel about insanity.

This is strange, if you think about it. You'd think the subject would give all sorts of people disastrous scope to write indulgent, carefully fucked-up prose asking us to think about whether the insane are actually more sane than the rest of us. Both Jennifer Dawson's *The Ha-Ha* and Clare Allan's *Poppy Shakespeare* miraculously avoid this horrible cliché; to crudify both of these terrific books, the line they take is that people suffering from a mental illness are more mentally ill than people who are not suffering from a mental illness. This, given the general use the subject is put to in popular culture, is something of a relief.

The Ha-Ha is a lost novel from 1961, recently championed by the English writer Susan Hill on her blog; *Poppy Shakespeare* was first published last year. Both are first novels, both are set in institutions, and both are narrated by young females attached to these institutions. *The Ha-Ha* is quieter, more conventional, partly because Jennifer Dawson's heroine is an Oxford graduate who speaks in a careful, if necessarily neurotic, Oxford prose. Clare Allan's N is a brilliant fictional creation whose subordinate clauses tumble over each other in an undisciplined, glorious rush of North London energy. I liked them both, but I loved *Poppy Shakespeare*. It's not often you finish a first novel by a writer and you are seized by the need to read her second immediately. Of course, by the time her

As you probably know by now – and more than eight million of you voted for it in the *Believer* Book Award – *The Road* may well be the most miserable book ever written, and God knows there's some competition out there. As you probably know by now, it's about the end of the world. Two survivors of the apocalypse, a man and his young son, wander through the scarred grey landscape foraging for food, and trying to avoid the feral gangs who would rather kill them and eat them than share their sandwiches with them. The man spends much of the book wondering whether he should shoot his son with their last remaining bullet, just to spare him any further pain. Sometimes they find unexpected caches of food and drink. Sometimes they find shrivelled heads, or the remains of a baby on a barbecue. Sometimes you feel like begging the man to use his last bullet on you, rather than the boy. The boy is a fictional creation, after all, but you're not. You're really suffering. Reading *The Road* is rather like attending the beautiful funeral of someone you love who has died young. You're happy that the ceremony seems to be going so well, and you know you'll remember the experience for the rest of your life, but the truth is that you'd rather not be there at all.

What do we think about when we read a novel this distressing? *The Road* is a brilliant book, but it is not a complicated one, so it's not as if we can distract ourselves with contemplation; you respond mostly with your gut rather than your mind. My wife, who read it just before I did, has vowed to become more practical in order to prepare herself for the end of the world; her lack of culinary imagination when handed a few wizened animal gizzards and some old bits of engine has left her with the feeling that she'd be an inadequate mother if worse comes to worst. And I ended up thinking about those occasional articles about the death of the novel – almost by definition, seeing as our planet hasn't yet suffered this kind of fatal trauma, you cannot find a non-fiction book as comprehensively harrowing or as provocative as this. Most of the time, however, you just experience an agonizing empathy, especially, perhaps, if you are a parent, and you end up wondering what you can possibly do with it, apart from carry it around with you for days afterwards. 'It is also a warning,' one of the reviews quoted on the back of my paperback tells me. Well, after reading this, I definitely won't be pushing the button that brings about the global holocaust.

It is important to remember that *The Road* is a product of one man's imagination: the literary world has a tendency to believe that the least consoling world view is The Truth. (How many times have you read someone describe a novel as 'unflinching', in approving terms? What's wrong with a little flinch every once in a while?) McCarthy is true to his own vision, which is what gives his novel its awesome power. But maybe when Judgement Day does come, we'll surprise each other by sharing our sandwiches and singing 'Bridge Over Troubled Water', rather than by scooping out our children's brains with spoons. Yes, it's the job of artists to force us to stare at the horror until we're on the verge of passing out. But it's also the job of artists to offer warmth and hope and maybe even an escape from lives that can occasionally seem unendurably drab. I wouldn't want to pick one job over the other – they both seem pretty important to me. And it's quite legitimate, I think, not to want to read *The Road*. There are some images now embedded in my memory that I don't especially want there. Don't let anyone tell you that you have a duty to read it.

So here's the introduction about mimicry. It goes something like this. Ahem. Believe it or not, I am not a good mimic. I can only do one impersonation, an actually pretty passable stab at Mick Jagger, but only as he appears in the *Simpsons* episode in which Homer goes to rock and roll fantasy camp. It's not much, I admit, but it's mine, and when I pull it off, my children laugh – simply, I guess, because it sounds so like the original, rather than because I am doing anything funny. (I never do anything funny.) Some of the considerable pleasure I drew from Eliza Minot's *The Brambles* was her enviable ability to capture family life with such precision that . . . Well, you don't want to laugh, exactly, because *The Brambles* is mostly about how three adult siblings cope with a dying father, but there is something about Minot's facility that engenders a kind of childlike delight. How did she do that? Do it again! One conversation in particular, in which a mother is attempting to explain the mysteries of death to her young children, is so loving in its depiction of the mess you can get into in these situations, and so uncannily authentic, that you end up resenting the amount of inauthentic claptrap you consume during your reading life. *The Brambles* isn't perfect – there's a plot twist that ends up overloading the narrative without giving the book anything much in return – but Eliza Minot is clearly on the verge of producing something special.

It's been a pretty significant reading month, now that I come to think about it. I read a modern classic that took away whatever will to live I have left, discovered a couple of younger writers and then came across an unfamiliar genre that, I suspect, will prove of great significance for both my reading and my writing life. I recently completed my first novel for, or possibly just about, young adults, and my US publishers asked me to go to Washington DC, to read from and talk about the book to an audience of librarians. One of the writers on the panel with me was a guy called David Almond, whose work I didn't know; a couple of days before I met him, his novel *Skellig* was voted the third greatest children's book of the last seventy years. (Philip Pullman's *Northern Lights* was top, and Philippa Pearce's *Tom's Midnight Garden* came in second.)

I read *Skellig* on the plane, and though I have no idea whether it's the third-greatest children's book of the last seventy years, I can tell you that it's one of the best novels published in the last decade, and I'd never heard of it. Have you? *Skellig* is the beautifully simple and bottomlessly complicated story of a boy who finds a sick angel in his garage, a stinking, croaking creature who loves Chinese takeaways and brown ale. Meanwhile, Michael's baby sister lies desperately sick in a hospital, fluttering gently between life and death.

The only problem with reading *Skellig* at an advanced age is that it's over before you know it; a twelve-year-old might be able to eke it out, spend a little longer in the exalted, downbeat world that Almond creates. *Skellig* is a children's book because it is accessible and because it has children at the centre of its narrative, but, believe me, it's for you too, because it's for everybody, and the author knows it. At one point, Mina, Michael's friend, a next-door neighbour who is being home-schooled, picks up one of Michael's books and flicks through it:

> 'Yeah, looks good,' she said. 'But what's the red sticker for?'
>
> 'It's for confident readers,' I said. 'It's to do with reading age.'
>
> 'And what if other readers wanted to read it? . . . And where would William Blake fit in? . . . "Tyger! Tyger! Burning bright / In the forests of the night." Is that for the best readers or the worst readers? Does it need a good reading age? . . . And if it was for the worst readers would the best readers not bother with it because it was too stupid for them?'

Now that I come to think about it, Mina's observations might well summarize what this column has been attempting to say all along.

For the first time in the last three or four years, I read two books in a row by the same author, and though *Clay* isn't quite as elegant as *Skellig*, it's still extraordinary, a piece of pre-Christian myth-making set in the north-east of England in the late 1960s. And suddenly, I'm aware that there may well be scores of authors like David Almond, people producing masterpieces that I am ignorant of because I happen to be older than the intended readership. Is *The Road* better than

Skellig? That wouldn't be a very interesting argument. But when I'd finished *Clay* I read an adult novel, a thriller, that was meretricious, dishonest, pretentious, disastrously constructed and garlanded with gushing reviews; in other words, the best readers had spoken.

Meanwhile, the hits just kept on coming. Gene Luen Yang's *American Born Chinese* is a clever, crisply drawn graphic novel about the embarrassment of almost belonging; Toby Barlow's *Sharp Teeth* is a novel about werewolves in Los Angeles, and it's written in blank verse, and it's tremendous. I can't remember now if I've ever cried wolf, as it were, and recommended other blank-verse werewolf novels – probably I have. Well, forget them all, because this is the one.

I was sent a proof copy of *Sharp Teeth*, and when I saw it, I wished it well, but couldn't imagine actually reading it, what with it being a blank-verse novel about werewolves and all. But I looked at the first page, got to the bottom of it, turned it over, read the second page and . . . You get the picture, anyway. You're all smart people, and you know the conventional way to get through a book. All I'm saying is that my desire to persist took me by surprise.

I had suspected that *Sharp Teeth* might not be serious – that it would turn out to be a satire about the film industry, for example (sharp teeth, LA, agents, producers, blah blah). But the beauty of the book is that it's deadly serious; like David Almond, Toby Barlow takes his mythical creatures literally, and lets the narrative provide the metaphor. It's stomach-churningly violent in places (they don't mess around, werewolves, do they?), and tender, and satisfyingly complicated: there's an involved plot about rival gangs that lends the book a great deal of noir cool. The blank verse does precisely what Barlow must have hoped it would do, namely, adds intensity without distracting, or affecting readability. And it's as ambitious as any literary novel, because underneath all that fur, it's about identity, community, love, death and all the things we want our books to be about. I'm not quite sure how Barlow can follow this, if he wants to. But there's every chance that *Sharp Teeth* will end up being clasped to the collective bosom of the young, dark and fucked-up.

It seems years ago now that I dipped into Joe Moran's engaging *Queuing for Beginners: The Story of Daily Life from Breakfast to Bedtime*. Externally, I have only aged a month or so since I picked it up, but in the meantime I have endured an Altamont of the mind, and my soul feels five hundred years old. Post-McCarthy, it's hard to remember those carefree days when I could engross myself in anecdotes about the Belisha beacon, and short social histories of commuting and the cigarette break. (Eighty-nine per cent of Englishmen smoked in 1949! And we were still a proper world power back then! My case rests.) And I suppose a sense of purpose and hope might return, slowly, if I read enough P. G. Wodehouse and sports biographies. I have nearly finished the Joe Moran, and I would very much like to read his final chapter about the duvet. But what's the point, really? There won't be duvets in the future, you know. And if there are, they will be needed to cover the putrefying bodies of our families. Is there anything funny on TV? ★

OCTOBER 2007

The story so far: I have written a Young Adult novel, and on a trip to Washington DC to promote it, I met a load of librarians and other assorted enthusiasts who introduced me to a magical new world that I knew nothing about. I really do feel as though I've walked through the back of a wardrobe into some parallel universe, peopled by amazing writers whom you never seem to read about on books pages, or who never come up in conversations with literary friends. (The truth, I suspect, is that these writers are frequently written about on books pages, and I have never bothered to read the reviews; come to think of it, they probably come up frequently in conversations with literary friends, and I have never bothered to listen to anything these friends say.)

It was in DC that I met David Almond, whose brilliant book *Skellig* started me off on this YA jag; and it was in DC that Francesca Lia Block's *Weetzie Bat*, first published in 1989, was frequently cited as something that started something, although to begin with, I wasn't sure what *Weetzie Bat* was, or even if the people talking about it were speaking in a language I understood, so I can't, unfortunately, tell you what *Weetzie Bat* is responsible for. When I got home, I bought it from Amazon (it doesn't seem to be available in the UK), and a few days later I received a very tiny paperback, 113 large-print pages long, and about three inches high, and suspiciously, intimidatingly pink. Pink! And gold! The book is so short that you really don't need to be seen with it on public transport, but I wouldn't have cared anyway, because it's beautiful, and I would have defended its honour against any football hooligan who wanted to snigger at me.

Weetzie Bat is, I suppose, about single mothers and AIDS and homosexuality and loneliness, but that's like saying that 'Desolation Row' is about Cinderella and Einstein and Bette Davis. And actually, when I was trying to recall the last time I was exposed to a mind this singular, it was Dylan's book *Chronicles* that I thought of – not because Block thinks or writes in a similar way, and she certainly doesn't write or think about similar things, but because this kind of originality in prose is very rare indeed. Most of the time we comprehend the imagination and intellect behind the novels we read, even when that intellect is more powerful than our own – you can admire and enjoy Philip Roth, for example, but I don't believe that anyone has ever finished *American Pastoral* and thought, 'Where the hell did that come from?' *Weetzie Bat* is not *American Pastoral* (and it's not 'Desolation Row' – or *Great Expectations*, while we're at it), but it's genuinely eccentric, and picking it up for the first time is like coming across a chocolate fountain in the middle of the desert. You might not feel like diving in, but you would certainly be curious about the decision-making process of the person who put it there.

Weetzie Bat is a young woman, and she lives in a Day-Glo, John Waters-camp version of Los Angeles. Eventually she meets the love of her life, whose name is My Secret Agent Lover Man, and they have a baby called Cherokee, and they adopt another one called Witch Baby, and . . . You know what? A synopsis isn't really going to do this book justice. If you've never heard of it (and of the six people questioned in the Spree offices, only one knew what I was talking about), and you want to spend about eighty-three minutes on an entirely different planet, then this is the book for you.

I read *Tom's Midnight Garden* because it finished one place above *Skellig* in a list of the greatest Carnegie Medallists of all time. (Philippa Pearce's classic came runner-up to Philip Pullman. I'm sure the Pullman is great, but it will be a while before I am persuaded that sprites and hobbits and third universes are for me, although I'm all for the death of God.) Like everything else in this genre, apparently, it is a work of genius, although unlike *Weetzie Bat* or *Skellig*, it is unquestionably a story for children, and at the halfway mark, I was beginning to feel as though I might finish it without feeling that my life had been profoundly enriched. I mean, I could see that it was great and so on, but I was wondering whether my half-century on the planet might be cushioning me from the full impact. But at the end of the book – and you've been able to see the twist coming from miles away, yet there's not a damned thing you can do to stop it from slaying you – I'm not ashamed to say that I cr—

Actually, I am ashamed to say that. It's a book about a kid who finds a magic garden at the back of his aunt's house, and there's no way a grown man should be doing that.

They've been very disorienting, these last few weeks. I see now that dismissing YA books because you're not a young adult is a little bit like refusing to watch thrillers on the grounds that you're not a policeman or a dangerous criminal, and as a consequence I've discovered a previously ignored room at the back of the bookstore that's filled with masterpieces I've never heard of, the YA equivalents of *The Maltese Falcon* and *Strangers on a Train*. Weirdly, then, reading YA stuff now is a little like being a young adult way back then. Is this Vonnegut guy any good? What about Albert Camus? Anyone ever heard of him? The world suddenly seems a larger place.

And there's more to this life-changing DC trip. While I was there, I learned about something called the Alex Awards, a list of ten adult books that the Young Adult Library Services Association believes will appeal to younger readers, and I became peculiarly – perhaps inappropriately – excited by the idea. Obviously this award is laudable and valuable and all that, but my first thought was this: 'You mean, every year someone publishes a list of ten adult books that are compelling enough for teenagers? In other words, a list of ten books that aren't boring? Let me at it.' I bought two of this year's nominees, Michael D'Orso's *Eagle Blue* and Ron Rash's *The World Made Straight*, having noticed that another of the ten was Michael Lewis's brilliant book about American football, *The Blind Side: Evolution of a Game*, and a fourth was David Mitchell's *Black Swan Green*, which I haven't read but which friends love. Whoever compiled this list knew what they were talking about. Who else might have won an Alex Award? Dickens, surely, for *Great Expectations* and *David Copperfield*, Donna Tartt, for *The Secret History*, Dodie Smith's *I Capture the Castle*, probably *Pride and Prejudice* and *Le Grand Meaulnes*. *This Boy's Life*, certainly, and *The Liars' Club*, Roddy Doyle for *Paddy*

Clarke Ha Ha Ha . . . In other words, if a book couldn't have made that list, then it's probably not worth reading.

Like every other paperback, Rash's book comes elaborately decorated with admiring quotes from reviews. Unlike every other paperback, however, his Alex nomination gave me confidence in them. 'A beautifully rendered palimpsest,' said *BookPage*, and I'd have to say that this wouldn't entice me, normally. You can see how a book could be a beautifully rendered palimpsest and yet somehow remain on the dull side. But the Alex allowed me to insert the words 'and not boring' at the end of the quote. 'Graceful, conscientious prose,' said the *Charlotte Observer* – and yet not boring. 'Rash writes with beauty and simplicity, understanding his characters with a poet's eye and heart and telling their tales with a poet's tongue, and not boring people rigid while he does it,' said William Gay, almost. You see how it works? It's fantastic.

And *The World Made Straight* really is engrossing – indeed, the last devastating fifty-odd pages are almost too compelling. You want to look away, but you can't, and as a consequence you have to watch while some bad men get what was coming to them, and a flawed, likeable man gets what you hoped he might avoid. It's a satisfyingly complicated story about second chances and history and education and the relationships between parents and their children; it's violent, real, very well written, and it moves like a train.

When I was reading it, I ended up trying to work out how some complicated novels seem small, claustrophobic, beside the point, sometimes even without a point, while others take off into the fresh air that all the great books seem to breathe. There would be plenty of ways of turning this book, with its drug deals and its Civil War backstory, into something too knotty to live – sometimes writers are so caught up in being true to the realities of their characters' lives that they seem to forget that they have to be true to ours too, however tangentially. Rash, however, manages to convince you right from the first page that his characters and his story are going to matter to you, even if you live in North London, rather than on a tobacco farm in North Carolina; it's an enviable skill, and it's demonstrated here so confidently, and with such a lack of show, that you almost forget Rash has it until it's too late, and your own sense of well-being is bound up in the fate of the characters. Bad mistake, almost. There is some redemption here, but it's real redemption, hard-won and fragile, rather than sappy redemption. *The World Made Straight* was a fantastic introduction to the Not Boring Awards. I was, I admit, a little concerned that these books might be a little too uplifting, and would wear their lessons and morals on their T-shirts, but this one at least is hard and powerful, and it refuses to judge people that some moral guardians might feel need judging.

Lawrence Weschler's *Everything That Rises: A Book of Convergences* is never going to be nominated for an Alex, I fear. Not because it's boring – it isn't – but it's dense, and allusive, by definition, and Weschler's thinking is angular, subtle, dizzying. I feel as though I only just recently became old enough to read it, so you lot will have to wait twenty or thirty years.

It's worth it, though. You know you're in for a treat right from the very first essay, in which Weschler interviews the Ground Zero photographer Joel Meyerowitz about the uncanny compositional similarities between his photos and a whole slew of other works of art. How come Meyerowitz's shot of the devastated Winter Garden in the World Trade Center looks exactly like one of Piranesi's imaginary prisons? Is it pure coincidence? Or conscious design? It turns out, of course, to be something in between, something much more interesting than either of these explanations, and in working towards the truth of it, Weschler produces more grounded observations about the production of art than you'd believe possible, given the apparently whimsical nature of the exercise.

And he does this time and time again, with his 'convergences'.

No, you think, in the first few lines of every one of these essays. Stop it. You are not going to be able to persuade me that Oliver Sacks's *Awakenings* can tell us anything about the recent history of Eastern Europe. Or no, Newt Gingrich and Slobodan Milošević have nothing in common, and I won't listen to you trying to argue otherwise. You got away with it last time, but this is too much. And then by the end of the piece, you feel stupid for not noticing it yourself, and you want Gingrich tried for war crimes. It's an incredibly rewarding read, part magic, part solid but inspired close practical criticism, and the best book about (mostly) art I've come across since Dave Hickey's mighty *Air Guitar*. When I'd finished *Everything That Rises* I felt cleverer – not just because I knew more, but because I felt it would help me to think more creatively about other things. In fact, I've just pitched an idea to Weschler's editor about the weird chimes between the departure of Thierry Henry from Arsenal and the last days of Nicolae Ceaușescu, but so far, no word. I think I might have blown his mind. ✱

NOVEMBER/DECEMBER 2007

Weirdly, I have had sackfuls of letters from *Believer* readers recently asking me – begging me – to imagine my reading month as a cake. I can only imagine that young people in America find things easier to picture if they are depicted in some kind of edible form, and, though one cannot help but find this troubling, in the end I value literacy more highly than health; if our two countries were full of fat readers, rather than millions of Victoria Beckhams, then we would all be better off.

As luck would have it, this was the perfect month to institute the cake analogies. The reading cake divided neatly in half, with Andrew Anthony's *The Fall-Out* and Ken Kalfus's *A Disorder Peculiar to the*

Country, both inspired by 9/11, on one plate, and Richard Russo's *Bridge of Sighs* and Lawrence Weschler's biography of the artist Robert Irwin on the other. Louis Sachar's *Holes*, meanwhile, is a kind of non-attributable, indivisible cherry on the top. There. Happy now? I'm warning you: it might not work that satisfactorily every month.

Andrew Anthony is a former five-a-side football teammate of mine (he still plays, but my hamstrings have forced me into a tragically premature retirement), a leggy, tough-tackling midfielder whose previous book was a little meditation on penalty kicks. I'm not underestimating Andy's talent when I say that this book is a top-corner thirty-yard volley out of the blue; you're always surprised, I suspect, when someone you know chiefly through sport produces a timely, pertinent and brilliantly argued book about the crisis in left-liberalism – unless you share a season ticket with Noam Chomsky, or Eric Hobsbawm is your goalkeeper.

Anthony (and if he wants a future in this business, he's got to get himself a surname) is a few years younger than I am, but we have more or less the same political memories and touchstones: the miners' strike in the mid-1980s, the earnest discussions about feminism that took place around the same time, the unexamined assumption that the USA was just as much an enemy of freedom as the Soviet Union. Liberalism was a dirty word, just as it is in America now, but in our case it was because liberals were softies who didn't want to smash the State. As Anthony points out, we would have been in a right state if anyone had smashed the State – most of us were dependent on the university grants or the dole money that the State gave us, but never mind. We wanted it gone. These views were commonplace among students and graduates in the 1980s; there were at least as many people who wanted to smash the State as there were people who wanted to listen to Haircut 100.

Anthony took it further than most. He read a lot of unreadable

Marxist pamphlets, and went to Nicaragua to help out the Sandi-nistas. (I would have gone, but what with one thing and another, the decade just seemed to slip by. And also, I know this keeps coming up, but what are you supposed to do when there's a revolution on and you're a season-ticket holder at a football club? Just, like, not go to the games?) He also had it tougher than most: Anthony was a working-class boy whose early childhood was spent in a house with-out a bath or an indoor toilet – a common enough experience in the Britain of the 1930s and 1940s, much rarer in the 1960s and 1970s. The things you learn about your friends when they write memoirs, eh? He had every right to sign up for a bit of class warfare. In the wearyingly inevitable name-calling that has accompanied the publi-cation of his book, he has been called a 'middle-class twat'.

Anthony, however, has concluded that the class war is now being fought only by the deluded and those so entrenched in the old ideologies that they have lost the power of reason. Which economic and political system would we really prefer? Which economic sys-tem would the working class prefer? Which economic system gives women the best chance of fulfilling their potential? Nobody, least of all Anthony, is suggesting that the free market should go unchecked – that's why liberalism still matters. Post 9/11, however, all that Old-Left aggression, now whizzing around with nowhere to go, is being spent not on Iran, or North Korea, or any of the other countries that make their citizens' lives a misery, but on the USA – not your hapless President, but the place, the people, the idea. Anthony threads some of the most egregious quotes from liberal-left writers throughout the book, and when you see them gathered together like that, these writers remind you of nothing so much as a bunch of drunks at closing time, muttering gibberish and swinging their fists at anyone who comes remotely close. 'It has become painfully clear that most Americans simply don't get it,' wrote one on 13 September 2001 (which, as Anthony points out, means that he would have had to have finished his copy exactly twenty-four hours after the Twin Towers fell). 'Shock, rage and grief there have been aplenty. But any glimmer of recognition of why . . . the United States is hated with such bitterness . . . seems almost entirely absent.' Yes, well. Give them another day or so to get over the shock and grief, and they're bound to come round to your way of thinking. 'When I look at the UK, it reminds me of the Nazi era,' said another, apparently in all seriousness. 'While the killing of innocent people is to be condemned without question, there is something rather repugnant about those who rush to renounce acts of terrorism,' said a third. (Are these rushers more or less repugnant than the acts of terrorism themselves? It's hard to tell.) By the time you get to the Index on Censorship editorial asking us to 'applaud Theo van Gogh's death as the marvellous piece of theatre it was', you start to wonder whether some of these people might actually be clinically insane. Van Gogh, you may remember, was the Dutch film-maker who was shot eight times and had his throat cut to the spine in broad daylight on a busy Amsterdam street. His last words were, 'Can't we talk about this?' How's that for censorship?

Sometimes, the doublethink necessary to produce observations and opinions like these can only produce disbelieving laughter. My favourite comic moment is provided by a leading Afro-Caribbean commentator, writing about the Asian immigrants expelled from Uganda by Idi Amin: 'The Asians from Uganda came to what can only be described as the most inhospitable country on earth.' The country he's talking about, of course, is Britain, the place the Asians fled to. This cannot literally be true, can it? However fierce our self-loathing, we must concede that, in this context at least, we came in a disappointing second place in The Most Inhospitable Country on Earth Cup. Uganda, the country that took everything the Ugandan Asians owned and forced them out under threat of death, won the gold medal fair and square.

This book has inevitably been misunderstood by many on the left as some kind of revisionist right-wing diatribe. It's true that Anthony owns up to believing in causes and systems that slowly revealed themselves to have been unworthy of anyone's belief, but this is an inevitable part of getting older. But *The Fall-Out* is really about the slippery relativist slope that leads tolerant, intelligent people to defend the right of unintelligent and intolerant people to be intolerant in ways that cannot help but damage a free society; I think we do a lot more of that in the UK than you do over there, possibly because the only people who have any real belief in an idea of England – invariably right-wing bigots – quite rightly play no real part in our political debate. Where is our Sarah Vowell?

Ken Kalfus's *A Disorder Peculiar to the Country* made a wonderful accompaniment to Anthony's book. You've probably read it already, so you know that it's about the frighteningly unpleasant, horribly believable end of a marriage, set during and after 9/11. The book opens with both parties having reason to hope that the other might have been killed, either in the Twin Towers or on a plane, and if you haven't read it already, then you will know from my synopsis of this narrative fragment whether you have the stomach for the rest of the novel. If the book has caught you at just the right point in your relationship, you'll wolf it down. And just in case my wife bothers to read this: I'm not talking about us, darling. At the time I wrote these words we were getting on well. I wolfed it down for entirely literary reasons. *A Disorder Peculiar to the Country* is a sophisticated piece of adult entertainment (and by the way, that last word is never used pejoratively or patronizingly in these pages), full of mess and paranoia and an invigorating viciousness, and it takes narrative risks, too – a rare quality in a novel that is essentially naturalistic and uninterested in formal experiment. Not all of them come off, but when they do – and the vertiginous ending is one that does, in spades – you feel as though this is a fictional voice that you haven't heard before.

So the plate with the other half of the cake on it was, like, an art plate, and I have to say that I haven't eaten it all yet. I'm two-thirds of the way through Russo's *Bridge of Sighs* and about halfway through Weschler's Robert Irwin book, and my suspicion is that I won't finish the latter. I'm so confused about the house rules that I'm really not sure whether I'm allowed to say that or not, even though it's a simple statement of fact; harbouring a suspicion that you won't finish a book is almost certainly a crime, and I'm almost certainly looking at a one-month suspension, but I don't care. My reluctance to finish the book is nothing to do with Lawrence Weschler – it's because I enjoyed *Everything That Rises*, his brilliant collection of essays, that I went out (or stayed in, anyway) and bought this one. It's more that the subject of his book is a minimalist artist, and when it comes to minimalist art, I am, I realize, an agnostic, maybe even an atheist.

I use these words because it seems to me that it's something you either believe in or you don't – a choice you're not really given with a Hockney or a Hopper or a Monet. Here's Irwin (clearly a likeable, thoughtful man, incidentally) on his late line paintings, which consist of several straight lines on an orange background:

> When you look . . . at them perceptually, you find that your eye ends up suspended in midair, midspace or even midstride: time and space seem to blend in the continuum of your presence. You lose your bearings for a moment. You end up in a totally meditative state.

Well, what if that doesn't happen to you? I mean, it doesn't happen to everyone, right? What are you left with? And it occurred to me that Catholics could make a similar claim about what happens when you receive Communion. There's a big difference between the body of Christ and a bit of wafer.

I shall write about Russo's absorbing, painstakingly detailed novel next month, when I've finished it. But I kept muddling up Irwin with Russo's artist character Noonan – not because the art they make is at all similar, but because the journey they take seems so unlikely. Noonan is a small-town no-hoper with a hateful father who grows up to be one of America's most celebrated painters; Irwin was a working-class kid from LA who loved cars and girls, went into the army and then embarked on an extraordinary theoretical journey that ends with the blurring of the space–time continuum. When you read about the two lives simultaneously, one adds credibility to the other.

Louis Sachar's *Holes* is funny, gripping and sad, a 'boy's own adventure' story rewritten by Kurt Vonnegut. Do you people ever do light reading, or is it all concrete poetry and state-of-the-nation novels? Because if you ever do take any time out, may I make a suggestion? These Young Adult novels I've been hoovering up are not light in the sense that they are disposable or unmemorable – on the contrary, they have all, without exception, been smart, complicated, deeply felt, deeply meant. They are light, however, in the sense that they are not built to resist your interest in them: they want to be read quickly and effortlessly. So instead of reading the ninth book in a detective series, why not knock off a modern classic instead?

P. S. Well, that didn't take long. I have been suspended for one issue. 'Wilful failure to finish a book,' it says here, 'thereby causing distress to a fellow author and failing in your duty to literature and/or criticism.' Ho hum. This has happened so often that it's water off a duck's back. See you in a couple of months. ✶

JANUARY 2008

I have recently spent two weeks travelling around your country – if your country is the one with the crazy time zones and the constant television advertisements for erectile dysfunction cures – on a fact-finding mission for this magazine: the Polysyllabic Spree, the forty-seven literature-loving, unnervingly even-tempered yet unsmiling young men and women who remove all the good jokes from this column every month, came to the conclusion that I am no longer in touch with American reading habits, and sent me on an admittedly enlightening tour of airport bookshops. This is how I know that your favourite writer is not Cormac McCarthy, nor even David Foster Wallace, but someone called Joel Osteen, who may even be a member of the Spree, for all I know: he has the same perfect teeth, and the same belief in the perfectibility of man through the agency of Jesus Christ our Saviour. Osteen was on TV every

time I turned it on – thank heaven for the adult pay-per-view channels! – and his book *Become a Better You* was everywhere. I suppose
I'll have to read it now, if only to find out what you are all thinking.

True story: I saw one person, an attractive thirty-something
woman, actually buy the book, in the bookstore at the George Bush
Intercontinental Airport in Houston, Texas, and, perhaps signifi-
cantly, she was weeping as she did so. She ran in, tears streaming
down her face and muttering to herself, and went straight to the
non-fiction hardback bestsellers display. Your guess is as good as
mine. I am almost certain that a feckless man was to blame (I suspect that she had been dumped somewhere between gates D15 and
D17) and, indeed, that feckless American men are generally responsible for the popularity of Christianity in the United States. In
England, interestingly, the men are not in the least bit feckless – and,
as a result, we are an almost entirely godless nation, and Joel Osteen
is never on our televisions.

I wrote this last paragraph shortly before going to the gym,
where for twenty minutes or so I wondered how to link the story of
the weeping woman to Tom Perrotta's *The Abstinence Teacher*; I just
couldn't see a smooth way of doing it. As *The Abstinence Teacher* is,
in part, about a feckless American male's rebirth as a Christian, I
ended my session on the cross-trainer wondering instead whether
my tour of US airport bookshops has left me brain-damaged. I am
almost sure it do has.

I should say that I read a UK proof copy of *The Abstinence Teacher*,
and that on the cover it claims that Tom Perrotta is an American . . .
Well, an American me. This is a high-risk, possibly even foolishly mis-
guided, marketing strategy, and does no justice to Perrotta's talent.
And it says a lot about my admiration for him, and my interest in
what he has to say on what puzzles those over here most about the
USA, that I overcame my initial dismay and wolfed it down – albeit

with the spine cracked, so that I could carry it around inside out. Needless to say, I end up absurdly flattered by the comparison: *The Abstinence Teacher* is a clever, funny, thoughtful and sympathetic novel.

Perrotta's initial focus is on Ruth Ramsey, a sex-education teacher who is having trouble with her school governors and the local evangelical church after telling her students, with a careless neutrality, that some people enjoy oral sex. When her daughter's soccer coach, a member of the church, leads the team in impromptu prayer after a victory, her outrage and grievance lure her into a confrontation that provides the bulk of the narrative, but what is particularly daring about *The Abstinence Teacher*, given Perrotta's constituency, is that he isn't afraid to switch point of view: it's all very well, and for Perrotta (I'm guessing) not particularly difficult, to give us access to the mind of a liberal sex-education teacher, but attempting to raise sympathy for a formerly deadbeat born-again Christian is another matter. Perrotta's Tim is a triumphant creation, though – believable and human. It helps that he's a burned-out ex-musician who's turned to the Lord to help him through his various dependencies – there but for the grace of God go the readers and writers of this magazine, and certainly half the potential readership of a literary novel. And Tim's nagging doubt is attractive, too. Where Perrotta really scores, though, is in his detailed imagining of his character's journey. It seems entirely credible, for example, that Tim should have a particular problem with Christian sex. He knows that the drugs and the alcohol were harmful, and are therefore best avoided. But seeing as he has to have sex anyway, with his naive and subservient Christian second wife, he cannot help but feel nostalgic for the old-school, hot and godless variety. I'm betting that this is exactly how it is for those who have followed Tim's path to redemption.

There was a similar collision between Christianity and liberalism in the cancelled TV series *Studio 60 on the Sunset Strip*, but it didn't make much of a noise, mostly because the Christian character – or, rather, her determination to appear weekly on a satirical liberal entertainment programme – constantly stretched our credulity, until our credulity tore right down the middle; Perrotta employs his considerable skill to ensure that Tim and Ruth are an accident waiting to happen.

Just recently, I read an interview with a contemporary literary novelist who worried – and I'm sure it was worry I heard in his voice, so the tone of lordly disdain was just mischievousness on the part of the interviewer – that books by me (and I apologize for repeatedly cropping up in this column as a writer, rather than as a reader) and other writers who use pop-culture references in their fiction would not be read in twenty-five years' time. And, yes, there's a possibility that in a quarter of a century, *The Abstinence Teacher* will mystify people who come across it: it's about America today, this minute, and it's chock-full of band names and movies and TV programmes. (One or two passages may mystify people who live in soccer-playing nations now, but I enjoyed the book too much to take issue with Perrotta about his failure to grasp the insignificance of the throw-in.) Yet some fiction at least should deal with the state of the here and now, no matter what the cost to the work's durability, no? This novel takes on an important subject – namely, the clash between two currently prevailing cultures opposed to an almost ludicrous degree – that is in urgent need of consideration by a writer as smart and as humane as Tom Perrotta. My advice to you is don't read writers with an eye on posterity. They are deeply serious people, and by picking up their books now, you are trivializing them. Plus, they're not interested in the money. They're above all that.

I have been writing this column for so long that I am now forced to consider a novel by my brother-in-law for the third time. Irritatingly, it's just as good as the other two, although it's a lot less Roman than either *Pompeii* or *Imperium*, which may or may not show some encouraging signs of failure and/or weakness. In fact, *The Ghost* is Robert's first novel set in the present day and, like *The Abstinence Teacher*, you don't want to wait twenty-five years to read it: it's about the relationship between Adam Lang, an ex-Prime Minister whose bafflingly close relationship with the USA has cost him a great deal, and his ghost writer whose research uncovers things that Lang would prefer remain covered up. As the two of them work together in a wintry Martha's Vineyard, Lang's world starts to fall apart. *The Ghost* is one part thriller, one part political commentary and one part the angry wish-fulfilment of an enraged liberal, and it has enough narrative energy to fuel a Combat Shadow. It also has a very neat GPS scene in it, the first I've come across in contemporary fiction. It has been said that Tony Blair is extremely vexed by *The Ghost*, so you don't even have to read it to feel its beneficent effects. If that's not a definition of great literature, then I don't know what is.

The last time I was here, I promised to return to Richard Russo's *Bridge of Sighs*, which I hadn't quite finished. Well, I finished it, and liked it (although not as much as I liked *Empire Falls*, which is an all-time favourite), and no longer feel competent to write about it. I started it on a sunlounger in France, and it's now November, and Lou 'Lucy' Lynch and his careful, gentle ruminations seem a lifetime ago. The same goes for Paul Zindel's *The Pigman*, this month's YA experience – I know I read it, but I'm not entirely sure I could tell you an awful lot about it. Maybe I should have done my book report the moment I finished it.

I recently discovered that when my friend Mary has finished a book, she won't start another for a couple of days – she wants to give her most recent reading experience a little more time to breathe, before it's suffocated by the next. This makes sense, and it's an entirely laudable policy, I think. Those of us who read neurotically, however – to ward off boredom, and the fear of our own ignorance, and our impending deaths – can't afford the time.

Speaking of which . . . Jeff Gordinier's forthcoming *X Saves the World* (subtitled *How Generation X Got the Shaft but Can Still Keep Everything from Sucking*) begins with an apposite quote from Douglas Coupland's novel *Generation X*:

> My life had become a series of scary incidents that simply weren't stringing together to make for an interesting book, and God, you get old so quickly! Time was (and is) running out.

X Saves the World starts with the assumption that the Boomers (born in the late 1940s and 1950s) have all sold out, and the Millennials are all nightmarish Britney clones who can't go to the toilet without filming the experience in anticipation of an MTV reality show. And that leaves Generation X, aka the slackers, aka the postmodern ironists, aka blah blah, to make something of the sorry mess we call, like, 'the world'. Gordinier, of course, is neither a Boomer nor a Millennial, which might in some eyes make his generalizations even more suspect than generalizations usually are, but I loved this book, anyway: it's impassioned, very quick on its feet, dense with all the right allusions – Kurt Cobain, the Replacements, Susan Sontag, Henry James and the rest of that whole crowd – funny and, in the end, actually rather moving.

And it's convincing, too, although of course it's hard to talk about generational mores and attitudes without raising all the old questions about when generations begin and end, and how we as a collection of individuals, as opposed to a banner-waving mob, are supposed to fit into it all neatly. As far as I can tell, I'm supposed to be a Boomer, but I was twelve when Woodstock took place, nineteen when *Anarchy in the* UK was released, and always felt closer to Johnny Rotten (and hence to everything that came after) than to David Crosby, so where am I supposed to fit into all this? There were Boomers that never sold out, plenty of Xers that did, and lots of lovable Millennials who worry about global warming and literacy levels. There have always been relentless and empty-headed self-promoters, although in the good old days we used to ignore them, rather than give them their own reality show. Gordinier is right, though, I think, when he argues that Generation X (and I know that even naming you like this makes me sound cheesy and square, but I can't say 'so-called' every time, nor can I raise my eyebrows and roll my eyes in print) has found another way of doing things, and that this way may well add up to something significant. This is a generation that not only understands technology but has internalized its capabilities, thus enabling it to think in a different way; this is a generation that knows that it can't change the world, a recognition that enables it to do what it can. Cinema, books, TV and music have all produced something new as a result, so long as you know where to look.

I suspect that those who write about Gordinier's book will engage him in his argument, and that very few people will point out how much fun this book is to read, but it is; the last chapter, which uses Henry James's novella *The Beast in the Jungle* and the life and work of James Brown as the ingredients for a passionate rallying cry, is particularly fizzy.

In other news: nearly a third of the football season is over, and Arsenal, still undefeated, are sitting at the top of the Premier League, despite having sold Thierry Henry to Barcelona in the summer. These are golden days, my friends, for another couple of weeks at least. This is how to become a better you: choose Arsène Wenger, Arsenal's brilliant manager, as your life coach. I did, and look at me now. If I found myself weeping in an airport, that's the book I'd buy: *Think Offensively, the Arsène Wenger Way*, but he hasn't written it yet. (You'll be reading about it here first if he ever does.) Mind you, even Joel Osteen would be able to see that we need a new goalkeeper urgently. ✶

FEBRUARY 2008

BOOKS BOUGHT:
* *The Raymond Chandler Papers: Selected Letters and Non-Fiction 1909–1959* – Tim Hiney and Frank MacShane (eds.)

BOOKS READ:
* *What Sport Tells Us About Life* – Ed Smith
* *The Absolutely True Diary of a Part-Time Indian* – Sherman Alexie
* *The Darling* – Russell Banks
* *The Rights of the Reader* – Daniel Pennac

The best description I know of what it feels like to learn to read comes in Francis Spufford's brilliant memoir *The Child That Books Built*:

> When I caught the mumps, I couldn't read; when I went back to school again, I could. The first page of *The Hobbit* was a thicket of symbols, to be decoded one at a time and joined hesitantly together . . . By the time I reached *The Hobbit*'s last page, though, writing had softened, and lost the outlines of the printed alphabet, and become a transparent liquid, first viscous and sluggish, like a jelly of meaning, then ever thinner and more mobile, flowing faster and faster, until it reached me at the speed of thinking and I could not entirely distinguish the suggestions it was making from my own thoughts. I had undergone the acceleration into the written word that you also experience as a change in the medium. In fact, writing

had ceased to be a thing – an object in the world – and become a medium, a substance you look through.

Firstly, we should note that the first book Spufford ever read was *The Hobbit*, a book that I still haven't picked up, partly because I am afraid I still won't understand it. Secondly, Spufford caught the mumps just as he turned six – he is one of the cleverest people I have ever come across, and yet some parents with young children would be freaking out if their kids weren't able to read by then. And lastly, I would just like to point out that you can't fake a memory like this. Learning to read happens once and once only for most of us, and for the vast majority of adults in First World countries it happened a long time ago. You have to dig deep, deep down into the bog of the almost lost, and then carry what you have found carefully to the surface, and then you have to find the words and images to describe what you see on your spade. Perhaps Spufford's amazing feat of recollection means nothing to you, but when I first read it, I knew absolutely that this was what happened to me: I, too, spooned up the jelly of meaning.

I turned back to Spufford's book because my five-year-old is on the verge of reading. (Yeah, you read that right, Spufford. Five! And only just! Francis Spufford was born in 1964 and this book was published in 2003, so by my reckoning my son will have produced something as good as *The Child That Books Built* by the year 2040, or something slightly better by 2041.) Writing hasn't softened for him: three-letter words are as insoluble as granite, and he can no more look through writing than he can look through his bedroom wall. The good news is that he's almost frenetically motivated; the bad news is that he is so eager to learn because he has got it into his head that he will be given a Nintendo DS machine when he can read and write, which he argues that he can do now to his own satisfaction – he can write his own name, and read the words Mum,

Dad, Spider, Man and at least eight others. As far as he is concerned, literacy is something that he can dispense with altogether in a couple of months, when the Nintendo turns up. It will have served its purpose.

Daniel Pennac's *The Rights of the Reader*, first published sixteen years ago in France, the author's native country, is a really rather lovely book about all the things parents and teachers do to discourage the art and habit of reading, and all the things we could do to persuade young people that literacy is worth keeping about one's person even after you've got it nailed. According to Pennac, we have spent most of our five-year-old son's life teaching him that reading is something to be endured: we threaten to withdraw stories at bedtime, and then never follow through with the threat ('an unbearable punishment, for them and for us', Pennac points out, and this is just one of the many moments of wisdom that will make you want him to be your adoptive dad); we dangle television and computers as rewards; we occasionally try to force him to read when he is demotivated, tired, bolshy. ('The lightness of our sentences stopped them getting bogged down: now having to mumble indecipherable letters stifles even their ability to dream,' says Pennac sadly.) All of these mistakes, it seems to me, are unavoidable at some time in the average parenting week, although Pennac does us a favour by exposing the perverse logic buried in them.

What's great about *The Rights of the Reader* is Pennac's tone – by turns wry, sad, amused, hopeful – and his endless fund of good sense: he likes his canon, but doesn't want to torture you into reading it, and rights 2 and 3 (the Right to Skip and the Right Not to Finish a Book) are, we must remind ourselves, fundamental human rights. The French book about reading that's been getting a lot of attention recently is Pierre Bayard's *How to Talk About Books You Haven't Read*, which should surely be retitled *You Need Some New Friends, Because the Ones You've Got Are Jerks*: literary editors seem to think it's zeitgeisty, but out in the world, grown-ups no longer feel the need to bullshit about literature, thank God. Pennac's book is the one we should all be thinking about, because its author hasn't given up. *The Rights of the Reader* is full of great quotes, too. Here's one of my favourites, from Flannery O'Connor:

> If teachers are in the habit of approaching a story as if it were a research problem for which any answer is believable so long as it is not obvious, then I think students will never learn to enjoy fiction.

That one is dedicated to anyone who graduated from college and found themselves unable to read anything that came from the imagination.

Russell Banks's *The Darling* was recommended to me – given to me, even – by the owner of a wonderful independent bookstore, Rakestraw Books, in Danville, California; booksellers know better than anyone that talking about books you have read is much more persuasive than attempting to sound smart about books you haven't. It's the second great novel about Africa by an American writer that I've read in the last year (I'm forbidden from talking about the other one by internal bureaucracy), although the creative impulse behind Banks's book is much tougher to read. It's in some ways a peculiar novel, in that it tracks the journey of a 1960s radical, the daughter of a famous paediatrician, as she travels all the way from the Weather Underground to war-torn Liberia, where she marries a local politician and takes care of chimpanzees. A crude synopsis is only likely to provoke the question, 'What the fuck?' But then, synopses are rarely much use when it comes to novels. Whatever prompted Banks to write *The Darling*, the material here provides him with an enormous and dazzling armoury of ironies and echoes, and his narrator, Hannah, by turns passionately engaged and icily detached, is inevitably reminiscent of a Graham Greene character. This is a novel

STUFF I'VE BEEN READING

that provides a potted history of Liberia, a dreamy, extended meditation on the connections between humans and apes, a convincing
examination of the internal life of an American refusenik and an
acute portrait of a mixed-race, cross-cultural marriage, and if you're
not interested in any of that, then we at the *Believer* politely suggest
that you'd be happier with another magazine.

I nearly didn't read Sherman Alexie's *The Absolutely True Diary of
a Part-Time Indian*, because I had decided that, as we had both had
Young Adult novels published at around the same time, we were
somehow in competition, and that his book was the Yankees, or
Manchester United, or Australia, or any other sporting nemesis
you care to name. And, of course, hearing that Alexie's novel was
great really didn't help overcome my reluctance – rather, it merely
hardened it. I'd like to think that by reading the book I have demonstrated some kind of maturity and come to recognize that books
are not like sports teams, and therefore can't play each other; mine
can't advance to the next round by dint of all-round physical superiority, no matter how thoroughly I coach it, no matter what diet I
put it on, no matter how many steroids I force down its little throat.
(If I thought that giving my novel performance-enhancing drugs
would help it in any way, I'd do it, though, and I'm not ashamed to
admit it.)

Anyway, *The Absolutely True Diary of a Part-Time Indian* is, as I was
told on my recent book tour by scores of unsupportive and thought-
less people, a terrific book, funny and moving and effortlessly
engaging. The part-time Indian of the title is Junior, a hydrocephalic
weakling whose decision to enrol at the white high school at the
edge of his reservation costs him both his closest friendship and
respect from his community. It's a coming-of-age story, but it's fresh:
I for one knew nothing about the world that Alexie describes, and in
any case Junior's voice – by turns defiant, worldly wise, sad and
scared – and Ellen Forney's cute and sympathetic drawings give the

book the feeling of a modern YA classic. And, seeing as the best YA fiction (see previous columns) is as punchy and engaging as anything you might come across in a bookstore, it's for you, too. If you see Sherman Alexie's novel getting a beating somewhere – in the ring, at a racetrack, or anywhere else you're likely to see books competing – then demand a urine test, because somebody's cheating.

I have written about Ed Smith before: his last book, *On and Off the Field*, was a diary of his season, and as he's a cricketer, I presumed that my banging on about a sport you didn't know, understand, or care about would annoy you, in a satisfying way. It's great, then, that he has another book coming out, this time a collection of essays dealing with the areas where sport (quite often cricket) is able to shed light on other areas of life. In the first essay he explains why there will never be another Don Bradman, but as you lot don't even know that you've missed the first Bradman altogether, it's a waste of time and column inches going into any further detail, so that's what I'll do. Bradman's batting average, the *New York Times* concluded in its 2001 obituary after some fancy mathematics, meant that he was better than Michael Jordan, Babe Ruth and Ty Cobb; nobody has got anywhere close to his record since, just as in baseball nobody has managed a .400 season since Ted Williams in 1941. (We weren't playing professional sports in 1941, you know. We were too busy fighting Nazis – an old grievance, maybe, but not one that anyone here is likely to forget for another few hundred years.) Smith argues that the increasing professionalism of sports means that it's much harder for sporting giants to tower quite as high over their peers: greater defensive competence and organization have resulted in a bunching somewhere nearer the middle. The bad players and teams are much better than they used to be, which means that the good ones find it harder to exert their superiority so crushingly. And when it comes to athletics, we can't get much faster, according to a Harvard evolutionary geneticist – 'the laws of oxygen exchange will not permit it'. Did you know that horses have stopped breaking racing records? They've now been bred to the point where they simply can't get any faster. I could eat this stuff up with a spoon.

You'll enjoy this: when the cricketer Fred Titmus made his professional debut, the tannoy announcer felt obliged to correct an error on the score card, 'F. J. Titmus should, of course, read Titmus, F. J.' An amateur player (a 'gentleman', in the class-bound language of cricket) was allowed to put his initials before his surname; a player – in other words, a professional – had to put his initials after. Titmus was being put in his place – in 1949. What a stupid country. This is why I have repeatedly turned down a knighthood. Knighthoods are no good to anyone, if they want to get on in Britain. I'm holding out for a lordship.

The chapter on what we can learn from amateurism (a word which, it's easy to forget, has its roots in the old-school, first-lesson Latin *amo amas amat*) is of value to pretty much any of us who have managed to end up doing what we love for a living. Anyone in this privileged position who has never for a moment experienced self-consciousness, or endured a bout of second-guessing, or ended up wondering what it was they loved in the first place is either mad or isn't getting paid a living wage (and now I come to think about it, pretty much every writer I have ever met belongs in one of these two camps); Smith's entertaining exploration of creativity and inspiration would be every bit as useful to a poet or a songwriter (and he ropes Dylan in to help make his case) as it would be to an opening batsman. Ha! So you might actually have to read this book about cricket! Even better!

Next month, apparently, this column will be entitled 'Stuff I've Been Watching' (for one issue only). I only watch *30 Rock* and *Match*

MARCH/APRIL 2008

FILMS WATCHED:
* *The Simpsons Movie*
* *Juno*
* *This Is England*
* *Unnameable*
* *I'm Not There*
* *And When Did You Last
  See Your Father?*

FILMS BORROWED FROM
POSTAL DVD LIBRARY:
* *Midnight Cowboy*
* *Downfall*

At first I was afraid. In fact, I was, indeed, petrified. 'Stuff I've Been Watching'? Are they sure? Even . . . this? And that? And if I own up, will they still let me write about stuff I've been reading? Or will the stuff I've watched count against me, on the grounds that anyone who watches either this or that is highly unlikely to know which way up you hold a book? I should admit straightaway that 'this' and 'that' contain no pornographic content whatsoever. 'This' is likely to be, in any given month, a football match between two village teams battling for a chance to play in the first qualifying round of the FA Cup; 'that', on the other hand, could very well be a repeat of a 1990s quiz show – *Family Fortunes*, say – broadcast on one of the UK's many excellent quiz-show rerun channels. This isn't all I watch, of course. There are the endless games between proper football teams, and the first-run quiz shows, but I'm not embarrassed about watching them. Like many parents, I go to the cinema rarely, because going to the cinema means going without dinner, and no film is worth that, really, with the possible exception of *Citizen Kane*, and I saw that on TV.

As luck would have it, however, I have been asked to write about stuff I watched in December, and in December I watch screener copies of movies on DVD. I am a member of BAFTA, the British Academy of Film and Television Arts, which means that at the end of the year, every half-decent film that might have half a chance of winning an award is pushed through my letter box. For free. The DVDs are piled high on a shelf in my living room, new films by Ang Lee and Paul Thomas Anderson, adaptations of books by Ian Mc-Ewan and Monica Ali, and they look . . . You know what? They look pretty daunting. Stacked up like that, they look not unlike books, in fact: already some of them are starting to give off the same slightly musty, worthy smell that you don't really want to associate with the cinema. Every year, some of them – many of them – will go unwatched. We're getting through a few of them, though. (And please welcome the first person plural pronoun to this column. Books are 'I', but movies are 'we', because that's how they get watched. Any views expressed herein, however, are mine, unless I manage to offend somebody in Hollywood with power and wealth, in which case that particular view was hers. She won't care. She's only an independent film producer.) So, from the top . . .

Just before Christmas, I was browsing the biography section of a chain bookstore, hopelessly looking for presents, when, suddenly and bewilderingly, the colour drained out of the book jackets: they had all turned sepia or white. I was almost certain that I'd been stricken by a rare medical condition until I realized that I had reached the section reserved for the genre known in the UK as the 'misery memoir'. These books, all inspired by the enormous success of Dave Pelzer, seem to deal exclusively with childhood hardship and abuse, and have titles like *Please Daddy, Put It Away*; the jackets are white or sepia, apart from a washed-out photo, because

Pelzer's books look like that. Anyway, in this chain bookstore, these memoirs had all been bunched together in a section called 'Real Lives' – as if Churchill or Katharine Hepburn or Tobias Wolff or Mary Karr had lived unreal lives.

I was reminded of the 'Real Lives' section when I was watching *This Is England*, a British independent film by the talented young English director Shane Meadows: there is a similarly hubristic claim to authenticity in the movie's title. Is the country depicted really England? Like, the whole of it? I've lived in England all my life, but I didn't recognize Meadows's version. He'd say that this is because I've spent my time in the soft south of the country, and he's made a film about the gritty north, and that's fair enough, although I'd be resistant to any argument that his England is more real than mine. What concerned me more is that some of the details on which any claim to authenticity must rest felt a little off to me. Why did the characters all have different regional accents, when the film is set in one depressed suburb of a northern English city? Were young no-hoper English skinheads really listening to Toots and the Maytals in 1983, or would they have stuck to their Madness and Bad Manners records? And did they really have instant access to the mythology of Woodstock when they were teasing their peers about clothes and haircuts? *This Is England* is a semi-autobiographical film about a twelve-year-old falling in with a dodgy crowd around the time of the Falklands War, when Margaret Thatcher's repulsive jingoism got roughly translated by some disenfranchised working-class kids into the violent and racist language of the far right. It's never less than gripping, not least because Meadows gets exemplary perform-ances from all his actors, especially thirteen-year-old Thomas Turgoose as Shaun. Any film that ends with the one black character being kicked half to death by a psychotic skinhead is always going to be hard to adore, but I'm glad I watched it.

We watched . . . Actually, I'd better just check something. Hey,

Spree! Do the same rules apply to movies as to books? We still have to be nice? Or say nothing at all? Yes? OK. So, we watched a film directed by a famous director, and starring famous people, and – as film agents say – we didn't love it. (Top tip: if a film agent ever tells you that he or she didn't love your novel or script, then you might as well kill yourself – because you're dead, anyway.) This particular film was about unpleasant people doing unkind things for increasingly contrived reasons, and though that's pretty much the dominant Hollywood genre, this one felt particularly phoney. It was gloomy and portentous, too, which is presumably why it's being pushed through letter boxes during the awards season.

I did, however, love Todd Haynes's clever, thoughtful, frequently dazzling meditation on the subject of Bob Dylan, *I'm Not There*, which, as you must surely know by now, stars Cate Blanchett as one of six actors taking on Dylan's various incarnations and personas. If you'd decided not to see it because it sounded gimmicky or just plain daft, then you should think again: I can't guarantee that you'll like it, obviously, but I'm positive that you won't dislike it on the grounds that Cate Blanchett and a fourteen-year-old black kid called Marcus Carl Franklin are being asked to interpret the career of someone who doesn't resemble them physically. On the contrary, one of the film's many triumphs is that you never question it for a second – or rather, any questioning you do is on the film-makers' own terms and at their behest, and as a consequence this helps you to engage with the endless complexity of both the material and Dylan himself.

None of these characters is called 'Bob Dylan'. Blanchett is Jude, the electric speed-freak *Don't Look Back*-era Bob (and her sections are occasionally reminiscent of Pennebaker's shaky hand-held documentary, when they're not borrowing from Richard Lester or *Blowup*); the character's name is suitably androgynous, and of course contains an echo of that famous 1966 taunt, which comes in handy when the moment arrives. Franklin plays a folk singer called Woody, who rides trains with hobos and carries around a guitar case bearing the familiar legend: This Machine Kills Fascists. 'It's 1959 and he's singing about boxcars?' a kindly woman who has taken Woody in and fed him asks witheringly, right at the start of the picture. 'Live your own time, child. Sing your own time.' This is a pretty good example of how Haynes has externalized and dramatized all the internal conversations Dylan must have had with himself over the last fifty-odd years, but it also provides the quest for all the characters: what and where is one's own time? Richard Gere's Billy the Kid is lost in a Pat Garrett/'Lily, Rosemary' Old West full of robber barons and the disenfranchised poor, and Jude, the most 'modern' of any of the versions available, ends up running back into his/her own head. Meanwhile Heath Ledger's Robbie, living in the here and now, splits painfully, *Blood on the Tracks*-style, from Charlotte Gainsbourg. So what use is the here and now, if all it can do is break your heart? Haynes has enormous fun with, and finds great profit in, the iconography of Dylan – there's so much of it that even a casual shot of a young couple huddled together against the cold, or a jokey montage scene showing Ledger bashing into a couple of dustbins while learning to ride a motorbike, teems with meaning. It's the best film about an artist that I've ever seen: it's meltingly beautiful and it has taken the trouble to engage its subject with love, care and intelligence. What more do you want? Even if you hate every decision that Haynes has taken, you can enjoy it as the best feature-length pop video ever made. Who wouldn't want to watch Heath Ledger and Charlotte Gainsbourg making love while 'I Want You' plays on the soundtrack?

There were two visits to cinemas this month: a family outing to see *The Simpsons Movie*, and a rare adults-only evening out for *Juno*. I can tell you little about *The Simpsons Movie* because – and I'm not big enough to resist naming names – Mila Douglas, five-year-old best friend of my middle son, was scared of it, and as her parents weren't with her, it was me that had to keep taking her out into the foyer, where she made a miraculous and immediate recovery every time. Scared! Of the Simpsons! I will cheerfully admit that I have failed as a father in pretty much every way bar one: my boys have been trained ruthlessly to watch whatever I make them watch. They won't flinch for a second, no matter who is being disembowelled on the screen in front of them. Mila (who is, perhaps not coincidentally, a girl) has, by contrast, clearly been 'well brought up', by parents who 'care' and who probably 'think' about what is 'age-appropriate'. Yeah, well. What good did that do her on an afternoon excursion with the Hornby family? From what I saw, the movie was as good as, but no better than, three average Simpsons episodes bolted together – an average Simpsons episode being, of course, smarter than an average Flaubert novel. It could well be, though, that I was sitting in the foyer listening to Mila Douglas's views on birthday-party fashion etiquette during the best jokes.

By the time you read this, there's probably a *Juno* backlash going on, and smart people are describing it as too cute and kooky for its own good. Well, I'm stuck in 2007, and in 2007 we still think that *Juno* is charming and funny and that Michael Cera is a comic genius. *Juno* also features the first but almost certainly not the last cinematic reference to a quarterly magazine based not too far from Believer Towers. We at the *Believer* are used to being talked about in the movies – there was a surprisingly well-informed conversation about our decision to take advertising in *Live Free or Die Hard*, and an affectionate spoof of the Spree in *Alvin and the Chipmunks*. It's about time our poor relations caught up.

I'm in the middle of watching *And When Did You Last See Your Father?* as we speak – I stopped last night just when I got to the bit about faecal vomit, but I'll watch Jim Broadbent die of bowel cancer this evening, if my morale is high enough. This movie was produced by a friend, directed by another friend and stars a third. It was adapted by a neighbour from a memoir written by a guy I see from time to time and whose book I admired very much. What do I think of it so far? I think it's brilliantly produced, directed, acted and written, and the source material is fantastic. Also, it's really good. ✷

course, is the fault of these fine authors or their almost certainly brilliant work. I was just itchy and scratchy and probably crusty, too, and I began to wonder whether I had simply lost the habit – the skill, even – of reading. I was beginning to feel that this one long, pained explanation would have to serve as my last in this space, which I would then simply hand over to someone young enough to plough all the way through to the end, or at least the middle, of anything they start. (Although isn't that supposed to be one of the problems with young people? That their brains have been so rotted by internet pornography and Nintendo that they are physically incapable of reading anything longer than a cereal packet? Maybe I will prove impossible to replace, and as long as I read a few opening paragraphs every month, this gig is mine for ever.) At least I have some facts at my disposal. Did you know that if you wrote out the human genome, one letter per millimetre, the text would be as long as the River Danube? Did you know that the most expensive living artist in 1876 was Meissonier, one of whose paintings went for nearly 400,000 francs? These are two of the many things I've learned by reading the beginnings of this month's books. I am beginning to think that this new regime will be ideal for my dotage. I can read the beginnings of a few books, sit at the bar at my local and regale people with fascinating nuggets of information. How can I fail to make friends if I know how long the human genome is?

Just as I was beginning to despair – and let's face it, a man who is tired of books is looking at an awful lot of *Rockford Files* reruns – a book lying on a trestle table in a local bookshop managed to communicate to me its desire to be read in its entirety, and I bought it, and I swallowed it whole. Quite why Graham McCann's *Spike & Co.*, about British comedy writing in the 1950s, should have succeeded in its siren call where scores of others failed remains mysterious. I had absolutely no previous desire to read it – I didn't even know it existed before the morning I bought it – and though

I love a couple of the writers McCann discusses, I hadn't thought about them in a long while. Maybe the book nutritionists are right (and I'm sure that those of you who live in California probably have book nutritionists working for you full-time, maybe even living in your ubiquitous 'guesthouses'): you need to listen to what your soul needs.

Spike & Co. is about a group of writers who formed a company called Associated London Scripts (they wanted to call themselves Associated British Scripts, but the local council turned them down on the grounds that they weren't big enough) who operated out of offices above a greengrocer's in Shepherd's Bush, and went on to change the course of British and American TV and radio writing. Out of these offices came the Goons, John Lennon's favourite radio show and a direct inspiration for Monty Python, *Steptoe and Son*, which became *Sanford and Son* in the USA, *Till Death Us Do Part*, known to you lot as *All in the Family*, and the sci-fi series *Doctor Who*, which is still running, in an admittedly snazzier form, today. I have known and loved these shows for much of my life, and yet I had no idea about the greengrocer aspect of it all, which seems to me extraordinary. Two of my favourite writers – and I'm not talking about writers of TV and radio comedy, but writers of all denominations – Ray Galton and Alan Simpson, met in a TB sanatorium, and I didn't know that, either. They were both desperately ill teenagers, neither expected to live much into his twenties; they met towards the end of their stay in the late 1940s, and by the mid-1960s had produced *Hancock's Half Hour* and *Steptoe and Son*, two series that have helped form the psyche of contemporary Britain. The chapter on Spike Milligan, meanwhile, provides an invaluable writing tip:

> Once he had started work on a script he disliked ever having to stop; he wrote as he thought, and if he came to a place where the right line failed to emerge, he would just jab a finger at one of the keys, type

'FUCK IT' or 'BOLLOCKS', and then carry on regardless. The first draft would feature plenty of such expletives, but then, with each successive version, the expletives grew fewer and fewer, until by about the tenth draft, he had a complete, expletive-free script . . .

I have found this more helpful than I am prepared to talk about in any great depth, possibly because I can build my own inadequacies right into the page, rather than let them hover around the edges.

I can't hope or imagine that you'll enjoy this book as much as I did. Much of it will be incomprehensible to you, and in any case, you're not me. John Carey points out in his book *What Good Are the Arts?* that there are millions of tiny decisions and influences, over the course of a lifetime, that help us form our relationships with books and music and the rest of it, and if you shared even half a dozen of them, I'd be surprised. Even if you'd bought the book at the same time at the same store, you couldn't have spent the previous hour on my analyst's couch – I would have noticed, because I'd have been lying on top of you. But as a direct result of *Spike & Co.*, two things happened: (1) I bought a signed commemorative Galton and Simpson print off the internet, and (2) I emailed a friend and asked him if he wanted to have a go at writing something with me, even though neither of us has TB or, indeed, any life-threatening infectious disease. *Spike & Co.* is a hymn to the joys of collaboration, and I suddenly became dissatisfied with the solitary nature of my day job. Such is the way of these things that nothing will come of it, of course, but we're having fun, and it's not often that you can say that about a day spent at a computer.

I read *The Shadow Catcher* and Junot Díaz's *The Brief Wondrous Life of Oscar Wao* because I had to: I agreed to judge the *Morning News's* Rooster competition, in which the best books of last year are drawn against each other in a knockout competition. At the time of writing, there is no overall winner, but I can tell you that Díaz unsportingly thumped Marianne Wiggins in my round. He's twenty years younger and, as far as one can tell from the jacket photos, a lot tougher than Wiggins, but he didn't let any of that stop him. I hope he's ashamed of himself. His book, incidentally, is brilliant.

The reading hiatus came during and after all the film watching but, luckily for you, I read a couple of books before it, so you can't leave just yet. Alec Wilkinson's *The Happiest Man in the World* is a study of Poppa Neutrino, and the book's title worked on me just as it was supposed to: I wanted to know his secret. I was once sent a self-help book called *Should You Leave?*, which was kicking around the house, in the way that books sometimes do, for months. Visitors would look at it, smile, pick it up, put it down and then eventually start flicking through it. Nobody actually asked which page contained the answer, but you could see that they were hoping to stumble upon it without looking as though they were trying. It strikes me that anyone caught reading *The Happiest Man in the World* is owning up to a similar sort of dissatisfaction. I'm not sure, though, that Poppa Neutrino, a kind of Zen hobo who has spent his life rafting across the Atlantic, inventing new football plays, etc., can provide the answers we might be looking for:

> He has begun to bleed constantly from his backside, so there is always a dark stripe down his pants . . .

> The box was six feet long, four feet tall and four feet wide . . . He came and went from the box only when no one was around, because he didn't want anyone to know he was living in it.

I was unable to put myself in Neutrino's position and imagine myself as anything other than thoroughly miserable, so I quickly gave up on the idea of discovering the route to my future happiness and looked instead for the source of his. This, too, remains elusive –

indeed, Poppa Neutrino seems to spend so much time starving, having heart attacks, living in boxes and bleeding from his backside that you can't help wondering whether there was a terrible mix-up, and whether the text belonging to this particular title is inside the cover of an altogether less promising-looking book. And there is a sleight of hand played here, too. The reason that many of us cannot live a life free of grinding obligation is because we have mortgages, children, parents, friends, and so on. Presumably the mortgage payments on boxes are not onerous, but Neutrino certainly has children, few of whom are mentioned at any great length; this raises the suspicion that it's easier to avoid grinding obligation if one simply chooses to ignore it. Those who read the *New Yorker* will know that Alec Wilkinson is incapable of writing anything dull or inelegant, and his obvious fascination with the subject gives the book a winning energy. That fascination, however, is not always entirely comprehensible.

The Happiest Man in the World made me think, though. Mostly I ended up thinking about the nature and value of experiences and memories, although I didn't get very far. Crossing the Atlantic on a raft or staying in to watch TV . . . It's all the same, in the end, isn't it? There comes a time when it's over, and all you can do is talk about it. And if that's the case, then . . . I'm sorry. If you bother with this column at all, it's probably because you're looking for book tips. You probably don't want to hear that all human endeavour is pointless.

Here's a tip: M. T. Anderson's *Feed*. This is yet another book that can be added to an increasingly long list entitled 'YA Novels I'd Never Heard of But Which Turn Out to Be Modern Classics', and *Feed* may well be the best of the lot. It's a sci-fi novel about a world in which everybody is plugged directly into a never-ending stream of text messages, shopping recommendations, pop music and movie trailers – this is metaphor rather than prediction – and as a consequence, Anderson's characters are frighteningly malleable and disturbingly inarticulate. Even the President of the USA has trouble with words! *Feed* is funny, serious, sad (there's a heartbreaking doomed romance at the centre), and superbly realized; the moment I finished it I bought Anderson's latest novel, which is completely different. (It's set in 1775, and it's about a boy who's raised by a group of rational philosophers, so it sounds like the author has allowed himself to be seduced by the promise of a quick buck.) I haven't even read the beginning of it yet, though. It's a novel, so I very much doubt there will be any interesting facts in the opening pages. I rather fear that I'm turning into my father. ★

SEPTEMBER 2008

If you were given a month to learn something about a subject about which you had hitherto known nothing, what would you choose? Quantum physics, maybe, or the works of Willa Cather, or the Hundred Years' War? Would you learn a language, or possibly teach yourself how to administer first aid in the event of a domestic accident? I ask only because in the last month I have read everything there is to read and, as a consequence, now know everything there is to know on the subject of the film version of *Doctor Dolittle*, and I am beginning to have my doubts about whether I chose my specialism wisely. (I'm talking here, of course, about the 1967 version starring Rex Harrison, not the later Eddie Murphy vehicle. I don't know anything about that one. I'm not daft.)

This peculiar interest happened by accident rather than by design. I read Mark Harris's book *Pictures at a Revolution*, which is about the five movies nominated for the 1967 Best Picture Oscar, and Harris's book led me to John Gregory Dunne's *The Studio*, first published in 1969. Inexplicably, *Doctor Dolittle* was, in the opinion of the Academy, one of the five best films – along with *The Graduate*, *Bonnie and Clyde*, *In the Heat of the Night* and *Guess Who's Coming to Dinner* – of 1967. (I say 'inexplicably' because I'm presuming the film was tosh – although this presumption is in itself inexplicable, because when I saw it, in 1967, I thought it was a work of rare genius.) In *The Studio*, a piece of behind-the-scenes reportage, Dunne was given complete access to the boardrooms and sets of Twentieth Century Fox, a studio that happened to be in the middle of making *Doctor Dolittle* at the time.

Fortunately, *Doctor Dolittle* is worth studying, to degree level and possibly beyond. Did you know, for example, that in today's money it cost $190 million to make? That Haile Selassie visited the set in LA, and Rex Harrison asked him, 'How do you like our jungle?' That the script required a chimpanzee to learn how to cook bacon and eggs in a frying pan, a skill that took Chee-Chee – and his three understudies – six months to acquire? (I'm pretty sure I picked it up in less than half that time, so all those stories about the intelligence of apes are way wide of the mark.) Some of these stories should be engraved on a plaque and placed outside Grauman's Chinese Theatre in Hollywood, as a monument to the stupidity, vanity and pointlessness of commercial movie-making.

Pictures at a Revolution is one of the best books about film I have ever read, and if you're remotely interested in the process of making movies – in the process of making anything at all – then you should read it. Of course, film-making has an enormous advantage when it comes to insider accounts, because every movie could have taken a different path, had crucial elements not fallen into place at crucial times. Robert Redford wanted to star in *The Graduate*; the writers of *Bonnie and Clyde* were desperate for Truffaut to direct their script, and Warren Beatty, one of the producers, saw Bob Dylan and Shirley MacLaine as the leads. (If only literature could be this interesting. You know, 'John Updike was scheduled to write *Catch-22* until right at the last moment. He pulled out when he was unexpectedly offered the first of the *Rabbit* books, after Saul Bellow's agent couldn't get the deal he wanted for his client . . .' As usual, books get stiffed with all the dull stories: 'He thought up the idea. Then he wrote it. Then it got published.' Who wants to read about that?) But Harris certainly exploits this advantage for all it's worth, and he does it with enormous intelligence, sympathy and verve. He builds his compelling plotlines through painstaking accumulation of minute detail, but never lets the detail cloud his sense of momentum, and the end result is a book that you might find yourself unable to put down.

Like the best of those non-fiction books that take a moment in time and shake it until it reveals its resonance, *Pictures at a Revolution* turns out to be about a lot of things. The subtitle indicates one of Harris's theses – that 1967 was a pivotal year in cinema history, the year that the old studio system started to collapse, to be replaced by an independent producer-led culture which still thrives today, although not all of these producers are making *The Graduate* or *Bonnie and Clyde*. Sidney Poitier's emergence as a star with real box-office clout allows Harris to weave the subject of race into his narrative. Poitier starred in two of these five movies, and only just avoided having to appear in *Doctor Dolittle*, too, and he ended up being attacked for letting his side down – the bland liberal pieties of *Guess Who's Coming to Dinner* were deemed particularly offensive – while living in fear of his life whenever he ventured below the Mason-Dixon line. Meanwhile, the influx of saucy European movies that had hip Americans flocking to the cinemas had put ruinous strain on the curious, church-controlled US censorship system, and Harris has fun with all the illogicalities and incongruities that were being backlit by the freedom of the 1960s: a bare breast was tolerable in *The Pawnbroker* because it was a movie about the Holocaust, but the naked girls in Antonioni's *Blowup* were unacceptable. Harris even finds room for the slow death of one form of movie criticism, as exemplified by the stuffy Bosley Crowther of the *New York Times*, and the sharper, fresher style that Pauline Kael introduced.

Pictures at a Revolution is smart, then, and it feels real, but these qualities are not what make it such an absorbing read – not for me, anyway. I should perhaps admit at this point that for the last four years or so I have been working on a film script, a labour of love that, like all such projects, occasionally looked as though it was unloved by anybody but me. To cut a long, boring, occasionally maddening and frequently depressing story short, it's now being made into a film, as we speak, and I'm sure that the sudden metamorphosis of script into movie made me relish this book even more than I might otherwise have done: on top of all its other virtues, *Pictures at a Revolution* captures perfectly the long, meandering, dirty and bewildering path from inspiration to production. There's no guarantee, of course, that anyone will ever see this film I've been involved in, but the great thing about Harris's book is that it has twenty-twenty hindsight, and it makes you feel as if anything might be possible. Who knew that the unemployable 29-year-old actor that Mike Nichols perversely cast in *The Graduate* would turn into Dustin Hoffman? Who could have predicted that the difficult young actress nicknamed, cruelly, 'Done Fadeaway' by Steve McQueen would turn out to be the Oscar-winning star of *Network*? In other words, this book creates the illusion of shape and destiny, always useful when you have no sense of either.

As an added bonus, Harris introduced me to a novel that turned out to be a neglected minor classic. Immediately before Anne Bancroft took the part of Mrs Robinson in *The Graduate*, she appeared in a small and apparently highly regarded British film called *The Pumpkin Eater*, adapted by Harold Pinter from a 1963 novel by Penelope Mortimer. It's a strange, fresh, gripping book, the story of a woman with five children by three different husbands, now married to a fourth, a successful scriptwriter named Jake Armitage, who is sleeping around. If the set-up stretches credulity, it should be pointed out that the plot is scrupulously, dizzyingly autobiographical. Or at least, Penelope Mortimer had a lot of children by several different men – not all of whom she was married to – before marrying the successful English novelist, playwright, scriptwriter and lawyer John Mortimer. One of the many achievements of *The Pumpkin Eater* is that it somehow manages to find the universal truths in what was hardly an archetypal situation: Mortimer peels several layers of skin off the subjects of motherhood, marriage and monogamy, so that what we're asked to look at is frequently red-raw and painful without being remotely self-dramatizing. In fact, there's a dreaminess to some of the prose that is particularly impressive, considering the tumult that the book describes and, presumably, was written in. Penelope Mortimer's books are mostly out of print, although the wonderful people at Persephone, a publisher that specializes in forgotten twentieth-century novels by women (*Miss Pettigrew Lives for a Day* is one of its notable successes in the UK), are bringing back a couple of them this year.

I'm sorry this section is so gossipy, but *The Pumpkin Eater* sheds an extraordinary light on a story that fascinated both the broadsheets and the tabloids in the UK a while back. In 2004 Sir John Mortimer, as he is now, was apparently surprised but delighted to learn that he had fathered a child with the well-known and much-loved British actress Wendy Craig at the beginning of the 1960s, while married to Penelope; father and son met for the first time in 2004, and have since formed a bond. (Imagine, I don't know, Garrison Keillor owning up to a child conceived with Shirley Jones of the Partridge Family and you will get a sense of the media interest in the story.) And yet in *The Pumpkin Eater*, Jake Armitage impregnates a young actress, just as his wife is being sterilized – a detail that sounds implausibly and melodramatically novelistic, but which is also, according to *A Voyage Round John Mortimer*, Valerie Grove's recently published biography, drawn from life. It is difficult to understand how his illegitimate son could have been a complete surprise to him, given that his wife had written about it in a novel forty-two years before he is supposed to have found out. If Sir John's surprise is genuine, then he is guilty of a far greater crime than infidelity: he never read his wife's stuff. This is unforgivable and, I would have thought, extremely good grounds for divorce. If I ever caught my wife not reading something I'd written, there'd be trouble.

I have read other things these last few weeks: Graham McCann's intelligent biography of Cary Grant; the great Richard Price's new novel, *Lush Life*, which is typically absorbing, real and breathtakingly plotted; Thurston Clarke's inspiring book about RFK's drive for the Democratic nomination in 1968, *The Last Campaign*. But I'm not going to write about them, because this is my last column in the *Believer*, at least for a while, and I wanted to leave some space to bang on about how much I've enjoyed the last five years. In 2003, when I began 'Stuff I've Been Reading', I hadn't read *David Copperfield* or Edmund Gosse's *Father and Son*. I'd never read a word by Marilynne Robinson, and *Gilead* hadn't been published. I hadn't read Dylan's *Chronicles*, *Citizen Vince*, *The Dirt*, *How to Breathe Underwater*, *Hangover Square*, *Feed*, *Skellig* . . . (And, on a more mournful note, two of my favourite contemporary writers, Lorrie Moore and Elizabeth McCracken, have managed to avoid being included in the 'Books Read' list through the simple but devious method of not writing anything since the column began.) I have been reading great books since I was sixteen or so, which means that I should have described one-seventh of my most memorable reading experiences in these pages, but it really feels like more than that: you, dear reader, have helped me to choose more wisely than I might otherwise have done, and to read a little bit more vigorously. And quitting (because, despite all the fist fights and legal problems I've had with the Polysyllabic Spree, they never did have the guts to fire me) worries me, because there must be a chance that I'll sink back into my old reading habits: until 2003, I lived exclusively on a diet of chick-lit novels, Arsenal programmes from the 1970s and my own books. At the moment, though, I am telling myself that I'm leaving because I want to read lots of Victorian novels that you wouldn't want to read about, a lie that lets me walk out with dignity and hope for the future. Thank you for listening, those of you that did – I'll miss you all. ✻

with this very issue on the website eHow.com. 'It's hard to turn your children away. The best thing a parent can do is help them understand that they are adults now and the rules have changed.' The new rules for parents, the piece goes on to say, should include charging rent and refusing to buy toiletries and other incidentals. I'm pretty sure I'm going to end up getting my own way on the incidental toiletries, should it come to that. It's pretty hot here at Believer Towers, and I suspect that the Polysyllabic Spree, the 115 dead-eyed but fragrant people who edit this magazine, will cave in long before I do. Still. It wasn't what I expected when I left – that eighteen months later, I'd be working for free deodorant. What's particularly humiliating in my case is that, unlike most boomerang children, I'm considerably older than those who have taken me back in. They're not as young as they were, the Spree, but even so.

I have decided to vent my spleen by embarking on a series of books that, I hope, will be of no interest whatsoever to the readership of this magazine. David Kynaston's superlative *Austerity Britain* is more than 600 pages long and deals with just six years, 1945–51, in the life of my country. The second volume in the series, *Family Britain, 1951–57*, has already been published, so I plan to move on to that next; Kynaston is going to take us through to Margaret Thatcher's election in 1979, and I'm warning you now that I plan to read every single word, and write about them in great detail in this column.

I am less than a third of the way through *Austerity Britain*, but I have read enough to know that this is a major work of social history: readable, brilliantly researched, informative and gripping. Part of Kynaston's triumph is his immense skill in marshalling the resources at his disposal: it seems at times as though he must have read every novel written in the period and every autobiography, whether that autobiography was written by a member of the post-war Labour government or by a member of England's post-war cricket team. (On page 199 of my paperback, he quotes from former Labour deputy leader Roy Hattersley, Stones bassist Bill Wyman and cookery writer Elizabeth David, all on the subject of the miserable, bitter winter of 1947.) And it goes without saying that he's listened to every radio programme, and trawled through every newspaper.

The effect Kynaston achieves is extraordinary: Britain changes month by month, like a child, and you end up feeling that every citizen of the world should have the opportunity to read a book this good about their own country. I'm glad that not everyone in the UK has read it (although it has sold a lot of copies), because you can steal anecdotes from it and pass them off as your own. One of my favourites so far is David Lean's account of showing *Brief Encounter* at a cinema in Rochester, Kent, to a tough audience full of sailors from the nearby Chatham dockyards:

'At the first love scene one woman down in the front started to laugh. I'll never forget it. And the second love scene it got worse. And then the audience caught on and waited for her to laugh and they all joined in and it ended in absolute shambles. They were rolling in the aisles.'

Brief Encounter is a much-loved British film, often taken out of a back pocket and waved about when someone wants to make a point about how we have changed as a nation, and what we have lost: in the old days, we spoke better, emoted less, stayed married, didn't get naked at the drop of a hat, etc. We are cursed with an apparently unshakeable conviction that we are all much more knowing than people used to be, back in the Pre-Ironic Age, so it is both instructive and humbling to learn that, half a century ago, Rochester sailors didn't need the *Onion* to tell them what was hilarious.

The best stuff of all Kynaston has taken from Britain's extraordinary Mass Observation project, which ran from the late 1930s to the mid-1960s. The creators of MO – the anthropologist Tom

Harrisson, the poet Charles Madge and the film-maker Humphrey Jennings, among others (even the formidable, and formidably clever, literary critic William Empson was involved somewhere) – got 500 volunteers to keep diaries or reply to questionnaires, and the results provide the best record of what the war and its aftermath meant to ordinary Britons. True, there were some peculiar types involved; Henry St John, a civil servant living in Bristol, scrupulously described each opportunity for masturbation, as and when it arose. A visit to London's Windmill Theatre, famous for its nude tableaux vivants, elicits this observation: 'I delayed masturbation until another para-nude appeared seen frontways, with drapery depending between the exposed breasts.' The day after Hiroshima sees Henry returning to a public lavatory in the north-east 'to see if I could masturbate over the mural inscriptions'. Say what you like about the internet, but for a certain class of underemployed male, life has become warmer and more hygienic.

It's not all about wanking, of course. *Austerity Britain* is about the morale of a battered, broke nation and its attempts to restore itself; it's about food rationing and town planning, housing and culture, socialism and aspiration, and it never forgets for a second that its (mostly grey and brown) tiles make up a big, big mosaic of our tiny, beleaguered island. And if you read or write fiction, you may be gratified to see how Kynaston relies on the contemporary stuff to add colour and authenticity to his portrait of the times. The received wisdom is that novels too much of the moment won't last; but what else do we have that delves so deeply into what we were thinking and feeling at any given period? In fifty or one hundred years' time, we are, I suspect, unlikely to want to know what someone writing in 2010 had to say about the American Civil War. I don't want to put you off, if you're just writing the last paragraph of a 700-page epic novel about Gettysburg – I'm sure you'll win loads of prizes, and so on. But after that, you've had it.

It's been a month of enjoyment in unlikely places, if David Kynaston will forgive me for wondering whether an enormous non-fiction book with the word 'austerity' in the title was going to be any fun. Francis Spufford's forthcoming novel, *Red Plenty*, is about Nikita Khrushchev's planned economy, and it contains the phrase (admittedly in the extensive footnotes at the back) 'the multipliers on which Kantorovich's solution to optimisation problems depended', and it's terrific. Yes, reading it involves a certain amount of self-congratulation – 'Look at me! I'm reading a book about shortages in the early 1960s Soviet rubber industry, and I'm loving it!' But actually, such sentiments are entirely misplaced, and completely unfair to Spufford, who has succeeded in turning possibly the least promising fictional material of all time into an incredibly smart, surprisingly involving and deeply eccentric book, a hammer-and-sickle version of Altman's *Nashville*, with central committees replacing country music. (*Red Plenty* would probably make a marvellous film, but I'll let someone else pitch the idea to the Hollywood studio that would have to pay for it.) Spufford provides a terrific cast, a mixture of the real and the fictional, and hundreds of vignettes that illustrate how Khrushchev's honourable drive to bring enough of whatever was needed to his hungry and oppressed countrymen impacted on the lives of economists, farmers, politicians, black marketeers and even hack writers. (There was, of course, no other type, seeing as you wrote what you were told to write.)

Francis Spufford's name has come up in this column before: his *The Child That Books Built* is a brilliant memoir about what we read when we're young and why. And though I am not alone in thinking that he has one of the most original minds in contemporary literature, there really aren't as many of us as there should be. His own fantastic perversity is to blame for this – apart from *Red Plenty* and the memoir, he's written books about ice and English boffins – but you always end up convinced that the fusty-looking subject he's picked is resonant in all sorts of ways that you couldn't possibly have foreseen. One of his themes here is the sheer brainpower required for the extraordinary experiment that was Soviet Communism; we know now that it was an experiment that failed, but controlling all aspects of supply and demand is a lot more complicated than sitting back and letting the market sort everything out. It turns out that genius is required. Even more than was necessary for the conception, research and writing of this extraordinary novel, but that's only because novels don't need as much as entire economic systems. Oh, come on. They really don't.

A year or so back, my co-editor and I selected a story by Philipp Meyer for a collection we were putting together. (It came out, this collection. It was one of the many money-making schemes of the last eighteen months that failed to make money. Short stories by mostly young, mostly unknown American writers! For publication in the UK only! What could have gone wrong? Nothing, that's what. Which is why I suspect that I've been diddled, and that my co-editor is currently snorting cocaine and buying racehorses in Florida.) It was pretty good, this story, so when I saw Meyer's first novel, *American Rust*, reviewed ecstatically in the *Economist*, of all places, I . . . well, I was going to say, self-aggrandizingly, that I hunted it down, like some kind of implacable bibliomaniac Mountie, but we all know that nowadays hunting books down takes about two seconds.

The cover of my copy of *American Rust* sports blurbs by both Patricia Cornwell and Colm Tóibín, which positions it very neatly: *American Rust* is one of those rare books that provide the reader with not only a big subject – the long, slow death of working-class America – but a gripping plot that tunnels us right into the middle of it. Isaac and Poe, early twenties, both have plans to escape their broken Pennsylvania town, full of rotting steel mills (the book is crying out for a quote from Springsteen to go alongside those from Tóibín and Cornwell). Isaac is smart, and wants to go to a California college; Poe has been offered a sports scholarship that he's too unfocused to accept. And then Isaac kills someone, and it all goes to hell.

There is nothing missing from this book that I noticed, nothing that Meyer can't do. His characters are beautifully drawn and memorable – not just Isaac and Poe, but the sisters and parents and police chiefs, even the minor characters, the Dickensian drifters and petty criminals that Isaac meets during his flight from Pennsylvania. The plot is constructed in such a way that it produces all kinds of delicate moral complications, and none of this is at the expense of the book's sorrowful, truly empathetic soul. And, unlike most first novelists, Meyer knows that we're all going to die, and that before we do so we are going to mess our lives up somehow. There. I hope that's sold it to you.

You have to admit that when three books this good get read back to back, I'm the one that has to be given most of the credit. Yes, I appreciate the craft that has gone into these books, the research, the love, the patience, the imagination, the immense skill – just as I appreciate the craft that goes into the making of a perfectly spherical and lovingly stitched football. But, with the greatest of respect to Kynaston, Spufford and Meyer, it's the reader who sticks the ball in the back of the net, the person who really counts. He shoots, he scores. Three times. A hat-trick, in his first column back! He's still got it. ✲

as anti-Oscar. *Austerity Britain*? That one's pretty obvious. Both words in that title are antithetical to everything that happens in Hollywood during awards season. You're unlikely to catch a CAA agent in the lobby of the Chateau Marmont reading Andrew Brown's thoughtful, occasionally pained book about his complicated relationship with Sweden; Elif Batuman's funny, original *The Possessed: Adventures with Russian Books and the People Who Read Them* is populated by people who spend their entire lives thinking about, say, the short stories of Isaac Babel, rather than Jennifer Aniston's career. (I'm not saying that one mental occupation is superior to the other, but they're certainly different, possibly even oppositional.) And even Patti Smith's memoir, which could have been glamorous and starry, is as much about Genet and Blake as it is about rock and roll, and is suffused with a sense of purpose and an authenticity absent even from independent cinema. Oh, and no fiction at all, which has got to be significant in some way, no? If you want to ward off corruption, then surely the best way to do it is to sit by a swimming pool and read a chapter about Britain's post-war housing crisis. It worked for me, anyway. I can exclusively reveal that if you sit by a swimming pool in LA, wearing swimming shorts and reading David Kynaston, then Hollywood starlets leave you alone.

Finishing *Austerity Britain* was indisputably my major achievement of the month, more satisfying, even, than sitting in a plush seat and applauding for three and a half hours while other people collected statuettes. A month ago I had read less than a third of the book, yet it was already becoming apparent that Kynaston's research, the eccentric depth and breadth of it, was going to provide more pleasure than one had any right to expect; there were occasions during the last few hundred pages when it made me laugh. At one point, Kynaston quotes a 1948 press release from the chairman of Hoover, and adds in a helpful parenthetical aside that it was 'probably written for him by a young Muriel Spark'. The joy that extra information brings is undeniable, but once you get to know Kynaston, you will come to recognize the pain and frustration hidden in that word 'probably': how many hours of his life, you wonder, were spent trying to remove it?

While I was reading about the birth of our National Health Service, President Obama was winning his battle to extend health care in America; it's salutary, then, to listen to the recollections of the doctors who treated working-class Britons in those early days:

> 'I certainly found when the Health Service started on the 5th July '48 that for the first six months I had as many as twenty or thirty ladies come to me who had the most unbelievable gynaecological conditions – I mean, of that twenty or thirty there would be at least ten who had complete prolapse of their womb, and they had to hold it up with a towel as if they had a large nappy on.'

Some eight million pairs of free spectacles were provided in the first year, as well as countless false teeth. It's not that people were dying without free health care; it's that their quality of life was extraordinarily, needlessly low. Before the NHS, we were fumbling around half blind, unable to chew and swaddled in giant home-made sanitary napkins; is it possible that in twenty-first-century America, the poor are doing the same? Two of the most distinctive looks in rock and roll were provided by the NHS, by the way. John Lennon's specs of choice were the 422 Panto Round Oval; meanwhile, Elvis Costello favoured the 524 Contour. What, you think David Kynaston would have failed to provide the serial numbers? Panto Round Oval, by the way, would be a pretty cool name for a band. Be my guest, but thank me in the acknowledgements.

My parents were in their twenties during the period covered in *Austerity Britain*, and it's easy to see why they and their generation went crazy when we asked for the simplest things – new hi-fis, Chopper bikes, Yes triple albums – when we were in our teens. They weren't lying; they really didn't have stuff like that when they were young. Some 35 per cent of urban households didn't have a fixed bath; nearly 20 per cent didn't have exclusive access to a toilet. One of the many people whose diaries provide Kynaston with the backbone to this book describes her father travelling from Leicester to West London, a distance of over a hundred miles, to watch the 1949 FA Cup Final, the equivalent of the Super Bowl back then. He didn't go all that way because he had a ticket for the game; it was just that he'd been invited to watch a friend's nine-inch black and white television. We stayed in the Beverly Wilshire for the Oscars, thank you for asking. It was OK.

I haven't read *Puzzled People*, the Mass Observation book published in 1947 about contemporary attitudes to spirituality, all the way through. (As I explained last month – please keep up – Mass Observation was a sociological experiment in which several hundred people were asked to keep diaries and, occasionally, to answer questionnaires; the results have provided historians, including David Kynaston, with a unique source of information.) And you don't need to read the whole thing, anyway. The oblique, first-person responses to metaphysical matters are ideal, if you have a spare moment to dabble in some found poetry – and who doesn't, really? – much as the surreality of the Clinton/Lewinsky testimony led to the brilliant little book *Poetry Under Oath* a few years back. ('I don't know / That I said that / I don't / I don't remember / What I said / And I don't remember / To whom I said it.') Here are a couple I made at home:

> The Purpose of Life
> Now you've caught me.
> I've no idea.
> My life's all work

And having babies.
Well, I think we're all cogs
Of one big machine.
What I'm wondering is,
What is the machine for?
That's your query.

Jesus
I wouldn't mind
Being like Him
But He was too good.
Didn't He say
'Be ye perfect'
Or something like that?
Well,
That's just
Ridiculous

I bought *Fishing in Utopia* because I found myself in a small and clearly struggling independent village bookshop, and I was desperate to give the proprietor some money, but it was a struggle to find anything that I could imagine myself reading, among all the cookbooks and local histories. And sometimes imagination is enough. Surely we all occasionally buy books because of a daydream we're having – a little fantasy about the people we might turn into one day, when our lives are different, quieter, more introspective, and when all the urgent reading, whatever that might be, has been done. We never arrive at that point, needless to say, but *Fishing in Utopia* – quirky, obviously smart, quiet and contemplative – is exactly the sort of thing I was going to pick up when I became someone else. By reading it now, I have got ahead of myself; I suspect that the vulgarity of awards season propelled me into my own future.

And in any case, the Sweden that Andrew Brown knew in the late 1970s and early 1980s is not a million miles, or even forty years, away from *Austerity Britain*. Our post-war Labour government was in some ways as paternalistic, and as dogged and dour in its pursuit of a more egalitarian society, as Olof Palme's Social Democrats, and one can't help but feel a sense of loss: there was a time when we were encouraged to think and act collectively, in ways that were not always designed to further individual self-interest. In England after the war, no TV was shown between the hours of 6 p.m. and 8 p.m., a hiatus that became known as the Toddlers' Truce. The BBC decided that bedtime was stressful enough for parents as it was; and, as there was only one TV channel in the UK until 1955, child-less viewers were left to twiddle their thumbs. In Olof Palme's Sweden, you bought booze in much the same way as you bought pornography: furtively, and from the back of a shady-looking shop. It would be nice to think that we have arrived at our current modus vivendi – children watching thirty-plus hours of TV a week, young people with a savage binge-drinking problem (in the UK, at least) – after prolonged national debates about individual liberty versus the greater good, but of course it just happened, mostly because the free market wanted it to. I may not have sold *Fishing in Utopia* to you unless you are at least a bit Swedish and/or you like casting flies. But Andrew Brown demonstrates that any subject under the sun, however unpromising, can be riveting, complex and resonant, if approached with intelligence and an elegant prose style. He even throws in a dreamy, mystical passage about the meaning and conso-lations of death, and you don't come across many of those.

Despite my affection for my German publishers, and for Cologne, the city in which my German publishers live, I wasn't particularly looking forward to reading at lit.COLOGNE, the hugely successful literary festival that takes place there every March. I had been trav-elling a lot (I was actually nominated for an Academy Award this year, believe it or not, and that necessitated quite a lot of schlepping around), and the novel I was reading from feels as though it came out a lifetime ago, and I hadn't written anything for the best part of a year. And then, the morning after my reading, I was in Cologne Cathedral with Patti Smith and our German editor, admiring the beautiful new Gerhard Richter window, and I remembered what's so great about literary festivals: stuff like that usually happens. It's not always Patti Smith, of course, but it's frequently someone interesting, someone whose work has meant a lot to me over the years, and I end up wondering what I could possibly have written in these twenty-four hours that would have justified missing out on the experience. I started *Just Kids* on the plane home and finished it a couple of days later.

Like Dylan's *Chronicles*, it's a riveting analysis of how an artist ended up the way she did (and as I get older, books about the sources of creativity are becoming especially interesting to me, for reasons I don't wish to think about), and all the things she read and listened to and looked at that helped her along the way. And it was a long journey, too. Smith arrived in New York in the summer of 1967, and her first album was released in 1975. In between there was drawing, and then poetry, and then poetry readings with a guitar, and then readings with a guitar and a piano . . . And yet this story, the story of how a New Jersey teenager turned into Patti Smith, is only a sub-plot, because *Just Kids* is about her relationship with Robert Mapplethorpe, the young man she met on her very first day in New York City, fell in love with, lived with and remained devoted to for the rest of his short life. One of the most impressive things about *Just Kids* is its discipline: that's Smith's subject, and she sticks to it, and everything else we learn about her comes to us through the prism of that narrative.

There is a lot in this book about being young in New York in the 1970s – the Chelsea Hotel, Warhol and Edie Sedgwick, Wayne County and Max's Kansas City, Tom Verlaine and Richard Lloyd, Gregory Corso and Sam Shepard. And of course one feels a pang, the sort of ache that comes from being the wrong age in the wrong place at the wrong time. The truth is, though, that many of us – most of us – could have been right outside the front door of Max's Kansas City and never taken the trouble (or plucked up the courage) to open it. You had to be Patti Smith, or somebody just as committed to a certain idea of life and how to live it, to do that. I felt a different kind of longing while reading *Just Kids*. I wanted to go back to a time when cities were cheap and full of junk, and on every side street there was a shop with dusty windows that sold radiograms and soul albums with the corners cut off, or second-hand books that nobody had taken the trouble to value. (Smith always seems to be finding copies of *Love and Mr Lewisham* signed by H. G. Wells, or complete sets of Henry James, the sale of which pays the rent for a couple of weeks.) Now it's just lattes and bottles of banana foot lotion, and it's difficult to see how banana foot lotion will end up producing the Patti Smiths of the twenty-first century; she needed the possibilities of the city, its apparently inexhaustible pleasures and surprises. Anyway, I loved *Just Kids*, and I will treasure my signed hardback until I die – when, like all my other precious signed first editions, it will be sold by my sons, for much less than it will be worth, probably to fund their gambling habits. And then, perhaps, it will be bought second hand by a rocking boho in some post-capitalist thrift store on Fifth Avenue or Oxford Street, and the whole thing will start up all over again. ✳

JULY/AUGUST 2010

If you are reading this in the USA, the presumption over here in the UK is that you have either just come out of a session with your shrink or you're just about to go into one, and for reasons best known to ourselves, we disapprove – in the same way that we disapprove of the way you sign up for twelve-step programmes at the drop of a hat, just because you're getting through a bottle of vodka every evening after work and throwing up in the street on the way home. 'That's just life,' we say. 'Deal with it.' (To which you'd probably reply, 'We are dealing with it! That's why we've signed up for a twelve-step programme!' So we'd go, 'Well, deal with it in a less self-absorbed way.' By which we mean, 'Don't deal with it at all! Grin and bear it!' But then, what do we know? We're smashed out of our skulls most of the time.)

Recently I read an interview with a British comic actress, an interesting, clever one, and she articulated, quite neatly, the bizarre assumptions and prejudices of my entire nation when it comes to the subject of the talking cure: 'I have serious problems with it . . . The way I see it is that you're paying someone, so they don't really care about you – they're not listening in the way that someone who loves you does.'

There's a good deal in that little lot to unpack. The assumption that if you give someone money, then, ipso facto, they don't care about you, is a curious one; the chief complaint I have about my dentist is that he cares too much, and as a consequence is always telling me not to eat this or smoke that. According to the actress, he should just be laughing all the way to the bank. And how does she feel about childcare? Maybe she can't bring herself to use it, but in our house we're effectively paying someone to love our kids. (Lord knows, it wouldn't happen any other way.) But the real zinger is in that second argument, the one about 'not listening in the way that someone who loves you does'. Aaaargh! Der! D'oh! That's the whole point, and to complain that therapists aren't friends is rather like complaining that osteopaths aren't pets.

One of the relationships described in *Who Is It That Can Tell Me Who I Am?*, psychotherapist Jane Haynes's gripping, moving and candid memoir, is clearly a defining relationship in her life, a love affair in all but the conventional sense. The affair is between Haynes and her own therapist, and the first half of the book is addressed to him; he died before their sessions had reached a conclusion, and Haynes's grief is agonizing and raw. So much for the theory that a bought relationship can't be real. In the second half of the book, Haynes describes the problems and the breakthroughs of a handful of her patients, people paralysed by the legacies of their personal histories, and only the most unimaginative and Gradgrindian of readers could doubt the value of the therapeutic process. Pills won't work for the patient whose long, sad personal narrative has produced an addiction to internet pornography; pills didn't work for the woman who was saved from suicide, tragicomically, only because of a supermarket bag she placed over her head after she'd taken an overdose. (The maid cleaning her hotel room would have presumed she was sleeping had it not been for the fact that her face was obscured by an advertisement for Tesco.) As Hilary Mantel says in her quite brilliant introduction, we don't enter the consulting room alone:

> . . . but with our parents and grandparents, and behind them, jostling their ghost limbs for space, our ancestral host, our tribe. All these people need a place in the room, all need to be heard. And against them, our own voice has to assert itself, small and clear, so that we possess the narrative of our own lives.

In a bravura passage, Mantel goes on to describe what those narratives might read like:

> For some of us, they are a jerky cinema flickering against a rumpled bedsheet, the reels out of order and the projectionist drunk. For some of us they are slick and fake as an old dance routine, all high kicks and false smiles and a desperate sweat inside an ill-fitting costume . . . For others, the narrative is the patter of a used-car salesman, a promise of progress and conveyance, insistently delivered with an oily smirk . . . There is a story we need to tell, we think: but this is not how; this is not it.

If you think you can find a friend who is prepared to listen hour after hour, year after year, to your painful, groping attempt to construct your own narrative, then good luck to you. Me, I have friends who are prepared to listen for ten minutes to my list of which players Arsenal Football Club needs to mount a serious challenge next year – but then, I'm an English bloke. My therapist, however, has tolerated more agonized, baffled nonsense than any human being should endure. And yes, I pay him, but not enough.

Perhaps unsurprisingly, given the tenor of Mantel's introduction and the nature of psychotherapy itself, with its painfully slow storyboarding of life's plot twists, there is a good deal in this book about the value of literature. Haynes repeatedly claims that she'd find her job impossible without it, in fact – that Shakespeare and Tolstoy, J. M. Barrie (there's an extraordinary passage from *Peter Pan* quoted here, hence its appearance in 'Books Bought') and Chekhov have all created grooves that our narratives frequently wobble into, helpfully, illuminatingly. So even if you have no time for Jung and Freud, there's something for the curious and literate *Believer* reader, and as I can't imagine there's any other kind, then this book is for you. It's occasionally a little self-dramatizing, but it's serious and seriously smart, and Haynes allows her patients a voice, too: Callum, the young man addicted to pornography, makes an incidental but extremely important observation about the 'pandemic' that the internet has helped spread among men of his generation. (Haynes quotes the psychoanalyst Joan Raphael-Leff, who says that sex 'is not merely a meeting of bodily parts or their insertion into the other but of flesh doing the bidding of fantasy'. So what does it say about those who use pornography, I wonder, that they are prepared to spend so much time watching the insertion of body parts?) I'm going to stop banging on about this book now, but I got a lot out of it. As you can probably tell.

In 1971, the Booker Prize suddenly changed its qualification period. Up until then, the prize had been awarded to a work of fiction published in the previous twelve months; in 1971 they switched it, and the award went to a book released contemporaneously. In other words, novels published in 1970 weren't eligible for the prize. So somebody has had the bright idea of creating a Lost Booker Prize for this one year, and as a consequence our bookstores are displaying a shortlist of novels that, if not exactly forgotten (they had to be in print to qualify), certainly weren't terribly near the top of British book-club reading lists – and I'm betting not many of you have read Nina Bawden's *The Birds on the Trees*, J. G. Farrell's *Troubles*, *The Bay of Noon* by Shirley Hazzard, *Fire from Heaven* by Mary Renault, *The Driver's Seat* by Muriel Spark, or Patrick White's *The Vivisector*. I bought three of them, partly because it was such a pleasure to see books published forty years ago on a table at the front of a chain store: British bookshops are desperately, crushingly dull at the moment. Our independents are almost all gone, leaving bookselling at the mercy of the chains and the supermarkets, and they tend to favour memoirs written, or at least approved, by reality TV stars with surgically enhanced breasts, and recipe books by TV chefs. To be honest, even memoirs written in person by reality TV stars with entirely natural breasts wouldn't lift the cultural spirits much. If asked to represent this magazine's views, I'd say we favour natural breasts over augmented, but that breasts generally are discounted when we come to consider literary merit. And if I have that wrong, then I can only apologize.

Nina Bawden's *The Birds on the Trees* is what became known, a few years later, as a Hampstead Novel – Hampstead being a wealthy borough of London that, in the imagination of some of our grumpier provincial critics, is full of people who work in the media and commit adultery. My wife grew up there, and she works in the media, but . . . Actually, I should do some fact-checking before I finish that sentence. I'll get back to you. Nobody would dare write a Hampstead Novel any more, I suspect, and though its disappearance is not necessarily a cause for noisy lamentation – there is only so much to say about novelists having affairs, after all – it's interesting to read an early example of the genre. *The Birds on the Trees* is about a middle-class media family (the wife is a novelist, the husband a journalist) in the process of falling apart, mostly because of the stress brought on by a son with mental-health problems. People drink a lot of spirits. Marshall McLuhan is mentioned, and he doesn't come up so much in fiction any more. There are lots of characters in this short book, all with tangled, knotty connections to each other – it feels like a novel-shaped Manhattan at times – and, refreshingly, Bawden doesn't feel the need to be definitive. There's none of that sense of 'if you read one book this year, make it this one'; you get the sense that it was written in an age when people consumed new fiction as a matter of course, so there was no need to say everything you had to say in one enormous, authoritative volume.

None of the Lost Booker books are very long; I chose to read Muriel Spark's *The Driver's Seat* (*a*) because I'd never read anything by Muriel Spark before, and she has the kind of reputation that convinced me I was missing out, and (*b*) her novel was so slim that it is almost invisible to the naked eye. And, if you look at the 'Books Bought' and 'Books Read' columns this month, you will see, dear youthful writer, that short books make sound economic and artistic sense. If Spark had written a doorstopper of a novel, I probably wouldn't have bought it; if I'd bought it, I wouldn't have gotten around to picking it up; if I'd picked it up, I wouldn't have finished it; if I'd finished it, I'd have chalked her off my to-do list, and my relationship with Muriel Spark would be over. As it is, she's all I read at the moment, and the income of her estate (she died four years ago) is swelling by the day. What's the flaw in this business plan? There isn't one.

My only caveat is that your short novels have to be really, really good – that's the motor for the whole thing. (If you're going to write bad short books, then forget it – you'd be better off writing one bad long one.) *The Driver's Seat*, which is pitched straight into the long grass somewhere between Patricia Highsmith and early Pinter, is a creepy and unsettling novella about a woman who travels from Britain to an unnamed European city, apparently because she is hell-bent on getting herself murdered. I couldn't really tell you why Spark felt compelled to write it, but understanding the creative instinct isn't a prerequisite for admiring a work of art, and its icy strangeness is part of its charm. *A Far Cry from Kensington* came later but is set earlier, in a West London boarding house whose inhabitants are drawn towards each other in strange ways when one of them, an editor at a publishing house, is rude to a talentless hack. (She calls him a 'pisseur de copie', an insult that is repeated gleefully and satisfyingly throughout the book. Spark is fond of strange, funny mantras.) *The Prime of Miss Jean Brodie* is her most famous novel, at least here, where the movie, starring Maggie Smith as an overbearing and eccentric teacher in a refined Scottish girls' school, is one of our national cinematic treasures. I probably enjoyed this last one the least of the three – partly because I'd seen the film, partly because Miss Brodie is such a brilliantly realized archetype that I felt I'd already come across several less successful versions of her. (Influential books are often a disappointment, if they're properly influential, because influence cannot guarantee the quality of the imitators, and your appetite for the original has been partially sated by its poor copies.) But what a writer Spark is – dry, odd, funny, aphoristic, wise, technically brilliant. I can't remember the last time I read a book by a well-established writer previously unknown to me that resulted in me devouring an entire oeuvre – but that only brings me back to the subject of short books, their beauty and charm and efficacy. *A Far Cry from Kensington* weighs in at a whopping 208 pages, but the rest are all around the 150 mark. You want your oeuvre devoured? Look and learn.

SEPTEMBER 2010

Four years ago to the very month, as I'm sure you will remember, this column daringly introduced a Scientist of the Month Award. The first winner was Matthias Wittlinger, of the University of Ulm, in Germany, who had done remarkable things with, and to, ants. In an attempt to discover how it was that they were able to find their way home, Wittlinger had shortened the legs of one group and put another group on stilts, in order to alter their stride patterns. Shortening the legs of ants struck us, back in 2006, as an entirely admirable way to spend one's time – but we were younger then, and it was a more innocent age. Despite the huge buzz surrounding the inaugural award, Wittlinger received nothing at all, and is unlikely even to know about his triumph, unless he subscribes to this magazine. And to add insult to injury, there was no subsequent winner, because the following month we forgot about the whole thing.

Anyway: it's back! I am absurdly pleased to announce that this month's recipient, Rolando Rodríguez-Muñoz, is employed at a university right here in England – the University of Exeter. Together with his colleague Tom Tregenza, Rodríguez-Muñoz has been studying the mating strategies of crickets; they discovered, according to the *Economist*, that 'small males . . . could overcome the handicap of their stature and win mates through prodigious chirping'. In other words, being the lead singer works for the nerdy and the disadvantaged in other species, too.

Rodríguez-Muñoz has shaded it over Tregenza because, after he and his colleagues had 'captured, marked, released and tracked hundreds of crickets', they filmed sixty-four different cricket burrows. Rodríguez-Muñoz then watched and analysed the results: 250,000 hours of footage. A quarter of a million hours! Just under three years of cricket porn! Presumably crickets, like the rest of us, spend much more time trying to get sex than actually having it, but even so, he must have seen some pretty racy stuff. Some of the sterner members of the judging panel tried to argue that because Rolando had watched the film on fast-forward, and on sixteen monitors at once, he had cut corners, but I'm not having that; as far as I'm concerned, watching crickets mate quickly is even harder than watching them mate in normal time. No, Rolando Rodríguez-Muñoz is a hero, and fully deserving of all the good things about to come his way.

There was a hurtful suggestion, four years ago, that the Scientist of the Month was somehow tangentially connected to the World Cup. He hasn't read enough to fill up a whole column, because he's spent the entire month watching TV, the argument went; so just because he stumbled upon an interesting article in a magazine between games, he's invented this bullshit to get him out of a hole. I resent this deeply, not least because it devalues the brilliant work of these amazing scientists. And though it is true that, at the time of writing, we are approaching the end of another World Cup, and reading time has, indeed, been in shorter supply, I can assure you that the sudden reappearance of this prestigious honour is pure, though admittedly baffling, coincidence.

The effect of the World Cup on the books I intended to read has been even more damaging in 2010 than it was in 2006. In '06, I simply didn't pick any up, and though I was troubled by the ease with which a game between Turkey and Croatia could suppress my hunger for literature, at least literature itself emerged from the tournament unscathed. This time around, as you can see from the list above, my appetite was partially satisfied by grazing on the first few pages of several books, and as a consequence, there are half-chewed novels lying all over the place. At least, I'm presuming they're lying all over the place; I seem to have temporarily lost most of them. When the World Cup is over, and we clear away the piles of betting slips and wall charts, some of them will, presumably, reappear. I wrote in this column recently about Muriel Spark's novels, their genius and their attractive brevity, but there is an obvious disadvantage to her concision: her books tend to get buried under things. I can put my hands on Dennis Lehane's historical novel *The Given Day* whenever I want, simply because it is 700 pages long. True, this hasn't helped it to get itself read, but at least it's visible. I didn't lose *The Girls of Slender Means*, and it was as eccentric and funny and sad as the bunch of Spark novels I read last month.

At the end of the last column, I vowed to have read *Our Mutual Friend* on an e-reader, and that didn't happen either. This was partly because of the football, and partly because the experience of reading

Dickens in this way was unsatisfactory. It wasn't just that a Victorian novelist clearly doesn't belong on a sleek twenty-first-century machine; I also took the cheapskate route and downloaded the novel from a website that allows you to download out-of-copyright novels for no charge. I helped myself to *Babbitt* and *The Adventures of Huckleberry Finn* at the same time. The edition squirted down to me came without footnotes, however, and I rather like footnotes. More to the point, I need footnotes occasionally. (You may well work out for yourself eventually that the 'dust' so vital to the plot is household rubbish, rather than fine grains of dirt, but it saves a lot of confusion and doubt to have this explained clearly and plainly right at the beginning of the novel.) The advantage handed the e-reading business by copyright laws hadn't really occurred to me before I helped myself, but it spells trouble for publishers, of course; Penguin and Co. make a lot of money selling books by people who are long dead, and if we all take the free-downloading route, then there will be less money for the living writers. In a spirit of self-chastisement, I bought a copy of *Our Mutual Friend* immediately, even though I have one somewhere already. It won't do any good, in the long run, because clearly books, publishers, readers and writers are all doomed. But maybe we should all do what we can to stave off impending disaster just that little bit longer.

I was attempting to read *Our Mutual Friend* for professional reasons: I'm supposed to be writing an introduction for a forthcoming edition. I read Colm Tóibín's *Brooklyn* for work, too: I was asked to consider taking on the job of adapting it for the cinema, and as about a million critics and several real people had told me how good it was, I took the offer seriously. It's not the best circumstance in which to read a novel. Instead of admiring the writing, thinking about the characters, turning the page to discover what happens next, you're thinking, 'Oh, I dunno,' and, 'Yay, I could chop that,' and, 'Miley Cyrus would be great for this,' and, 'Do I really want to spend the next few years of my life wrecking this guy's prose?' It is a tribute to Tóibín's novel – its quiet, careful prose, its almost agonizing empathy for its characters, its conviction in its own reality – that pretty soon I forgot why I was reading it, and just read it. And then, after I'd finished it, I decided that I wanted to adapt it – not just because I loved it, but because I could see it. Not the movie, necessarily, but the world of the novel: the third-class cabin in which his protagonist travels from Liverpool to New York in the early 1950s, the department store she works in, the dances she attends. They are portrayed with a director of photography's relish for depth and light and detail.

The laziest, most irritating book-club criticism of a novel is that the reader 'just didn't care' about the characters or their predicament, a complaint usually made in a tone suggesting that this banality is the product of deep and original thought. (It never seems to occur to these critics that the deficiency may well lie within themselves, rather than in the pages of the books. Perhaps they feel similarly about their friends, parents, children. 'The trouble with my kid is that she doesn't make me care enough about her.' Are we all supposed to nod sagely at that?)

It is not intended to be a backhanded compliment when I say that Tóibín doesn't care whether you care about Eilis, his heroine; it's not that the book is chilly or neutral, or that Tóibín is a disengaged writer. He's not. But he's patient, and nerveless, and unsentimental, and he trusts the story rather than the prose to deliver the emotional pay-off. And it does deliver. *Brooklyn* chooses the narrative form of a much cheaper kind of book – 'one woman, two countries, two men' – but that isn't what it's about; you're not quite sure what it's about until the last few pages, and then you can see how carefully the trap has been laid for you. I loved it. Will I wreck it? It's perfectly possible, of course. It's a very delicate piece, and Eilis is a watchful, still centre. I won't have to hack away at its complicated architecture, though, because it doesn't have one, so maybe I have half a chance. By the time you read this, I should have started in on it; if you have a ten-year-old daughter with ambitions to be an actor, then she might as well start trying to acquire an Irish accent. In my experience of the film business, we'll be shooting sometime in 2020, if it hasn't all collapsed by then.

In a way, I read *Live from New York*, an oral history of *Saturday Night Live*, because of work, too. Earlier in the year I got an American agent, a lovely, smart woman whose every idea, suggestion and request I've ignored, more or less since the moment we agreed she'd represent me. Anyway, she recommended Tom Shales and James Andrew Miller's book, and my feeling was that if I'm not going to make her a penny, I could at least follow up on her book tips. And I'm pretty sure that if it had to be one or the other, money or successful recommendations, she'd go for the recommendations. That's what makes her special.

I read the book despite never having seen a single minute of *Saturday Night Live*, at least prior to Tina Fey's turn as Sarah Palin in 2008. The show was never shown in the UK, so I hadn't a clue who any of these people were. Will Ferrell? Bill Murray? Adam Sandler? Eddie Murphy? John Belushi? Chris Rock? Dan Aykroyd? It's sweet that you have your own TV stars over there. You've probably never heard of Pat Phoenix, either.

When it's done well, as it is here, then the oral history is pretty unbeatable as a non-fiction form – engrossing, light on its feet, the constant switching of voices a guarantee against dullness. Legs McNeil and Gillian McCain's *Please Kill Me: The Uncensored Oral History of Punk*, Jean Stein and George Plimpton's Edie Sedgwick book, Studs Terkel's *Working* . . . These are books that I hope to return to one day, when I've read everything else. *Live from New York* is probably just a little too long for someone unfamiliar with the show, but if you want to learn something about the crafts of writing and performing, then you'll pick something up every few pages. I am still thinking about these words from Lorne Michaels:

> The amount of things that have to come together for something to be good is just staggering. And the fact that there's anything good at all is just amazing. When you're young, you assume that just knowing the difference between good and bad is enough: 'I'll just do good work, because I prefer it to bad work.'

Michaels's observation contains a terrible truth: you think, at a certain point in your life, that your impeccable taste will save you. As life goes on, you realize it's a bit more complicated than that.

While I was reading *Live from New York*, I realized that G. E. Smith, the show's musical director, was the same G. E. Smith who sat next to me on a plane from New York to London, sometime in 1976 or 1977. I was just returning to college after visiting my dad; Smith was on tour with Daryl Hall and John Oates, who were up in first class. He was the first musician I'd ever met, and he was charming and generous with his time. And he sold me on *Abandoned Luncheonette*, Hall and Oates's heart-stoppingly lovely folk-soul album, recorded well before the disco years (which were pretty good, too, actually). He wouldn't remember a single second of them, but the conversations we had on that flight helped feed the idea, just sprouting then, that I didn't want a proper job. It was a pretty seminal flight, now that I come to think about it. I still love *Abandoned Luncheonette*. ✭

OCTOBER 2010

On the day I arrived at last year's Sundance Film Festival, amid the snow and the painfully cold sponsored parties, I met a screenwriter who wanted to talk, not about movies or agents or distribution deals, but about this column, and this column only. Given the happy relationship between books and film, and the mutual understanding between authors and those who work in the movie industry, I presumed that this would be the first of many such conversations about the *Believer*; indeed, I was afraid that, after a couple of days, I would begin to tire of the subject. I didn't want to be asked, over and over again, what the members of the Polysyllabic Spree were really like, in real life; I wanted the chance to offer my opinion on Miramax's troubles, or the potential weaknesses in the new set-up at WME. I made it my policy from that moment on to engage only with people who didn't look like *Believer* readers. It was a policy that proved to be amazingly successful.

So Michael was the one who slipped under the wire, and I'm glad he did. He wanted one shot at a book recommendation – presumably on the basis of the fact that my own had ruined his reading life over the last few years – and hit me with John Williams's novel *Stoner*. (To my relief, the title turned out to refer to a surname rather than an occupation.) *Stoner* is a brilliant, beautiful, inexorably sad, wise and elegant novel, one of the best I read during my grotesquely unfair suspension from these pages. So when Michael, emboldened by his triumph, came back with a second tip, I listened, and I bought.

Don Carpenter's *Hard Rain Falling* is, like *Stoner*, part of the NYRB Classics series, but it didn't begin its life, back in 1966, wearing that sort of smart hat. Search the title in Google Images and you'll find a couple of the original covers, neither of which give the impression that Carpenter could read, let alone write. One shows a very bad drawing of a hunky bad boy leaning against the door of his jail cell; the other is a little murky on my screen, but I'm pretty sure I can see supine nudity. And, of course, these illustrations misrepresent Carpenter's talents and intentions, but they don't entirely misrepresent his novel: if you'd paid good money for it back in 1966, in the hope that (in the immortal words of Mervyn Griffith-Jones, the hapless chief prosecutor at the *Lady Chatterley* trial in 1960) you might be picking up something that you wouldn't want your wife and servants to read, then you wouldn't have asked for your money back.

A lot of books containing descriptions of sex have been written since the 1960s, and I pride myself on having read at least part of every single one of them, but there was something about Carpenter's novel that dated the dirty bits, and sent me right back to my 1960s childhood. Every now and again, I would, if I delved deep enough in the right drawers, come across books that my father had hidden carefully away – John Cleland's *Fanny Hill*, for example, first published in 1749, but still being read surreptitiously, in the UK at least, over 200 years later. (Wikipedia tells me that *Fanny Hill* was banned in the UK until 1970, but I found the family edition long before that, so I don't know where my father got his copy. He has gone up even further in my estimation.) We are long past the time when literature was capable of doubling as pornography, and I doubt whether twenty-first-century teenage boys with access to a computer bother riffling through *The Godfather* and Harold Robbins paperbacks as assiduously as I did in the early seventies. These days, regrettably, sex in novels must contain a justifying subtext; what dates the coupling in Carpenter's novel is that, some of the time at least, the couples concerned are simply enjoying themselves. I can't remember the last time I read a description in a literary novel of a couple doing it just for fun. (And if you have written exactly such a novel yourself, I am happy for you, and congratulations, but please don't send it to me. It's too late now.)

Hard Rain Falling is a hard-boiled juvenile-delinquent novel, and then a prison novel, and then a dark Yatesian novel of existential marital despair, and just about every metamorphosis is compelling, rich, dark but not airless. Carpenter is, at his best, a dramatist: whenever there is conflict, minor characters, dialogue, people in a pool-hall or a cell or a bed, his novel comes thrillingly alive. The energy levels, both mine and the book's, dipped a little when Carpenter's protagonist, Jack Levitt, finds himself in solitary confinement, where he is prone to long bouts of sometimes crazed introspection. Form and content are matched perfectly in these passages, but that doesn't make them any more fun to read. Most of the time, though, *Hard Rain Falling* is terrific – and if you're reading this, Michael, then I'd like you to know you have earned a third recommendation.

I finished *Hard Rain Falling* in Dorset, in a wonderful disused hotel which pitches its atmosphere halfway between Fawlty Towers and *The Shining*'s Overlook. I was there with family and friends; and, though I never forgot that I am a reader – I read, which helped to remind me – I completely forgot that I am a writer. This meant that the flavour of *The Conversations*, a collection of Michael Ondaatje's erudite, stimulating, surprising interviews with the film editor Walter Murch, was different from what it would have been had I devoured it during the rest of the year. In these pages a couple of months ago, I said that books about creativity and its sources are becoming increasingly important to me as I get older, but this has to be something connected with work – when I read these books (Patti Smith's memoir was the most recent, I think) I try to twist them into a shape that makes some kind of sense to me professionally. There is so much that is of value to writers in *The Conversations*; any book about film editing that manages to find room for the first and last drafts of Elizabeth Bishop's 'One Art', in their entirety, has an ambition and a scope that elude most books about poetry. If I'd been in a different mode – in the middle of a novel, say – I'd have been much more alert to the book's value as a professional aid; and just occasionally, something that one of these two clever men said would jerk me out of my vacation and back to my computer all those miles away. Murch's reference to 'Negative Twenty Questions', for example, a game invented by the quantum physicist John Wheeler to explain how the world looks at a quantum level (and much too complicated to tell you about here . . .), something about the way Murch used the game to illustrate the process of film editing dimly reminded me of how writing a book feels, if you end up plotting on the hoof.

But mostly I read the book simply as someone who has seen a lot of films, and as Murch edited *Apocalypse Now* and *The Godfather* and *The Conversation* and *The English Patient* (and re-edited Welles's *Touch of Evil* using the fifty-eight-page memo that Welles wrote to the studio after he'd seen the studio's cut of the film), then I was in experienced hands: this book is a dream, not just for cineastes, but for anyone interested in the tiny but crucial creative decisions that go into the making of anything at all. At one point, Murch talks about recording the sound of a door closing in *The Godfather* – a film, you suddenly remember, whose entire meaning rests on the sound of a door closing, when Michael excludes Diane Keaton from the world he promised he'd never join. If Murch had gotten that wrong, and the door had closed with a weedy, phoney click, then it's entirely possible that we wouldn't still be reading about his career today. And there's tons of stuff like that, discussions that seem like the nerdy fetishization of trivia, until the import of that trivia becomes clear. Harry Caul in *The Conversation* was going to be called Harry Caller (after *Steppenwolf*'s Harry Haller), until he decided that 'Caller' was an insufficiently oblique name for a professional bugger. So 'Caller' became 'Call', which became 'Caul' after a secretary's misprint, which in turn gave Coppola the idea of dressing Gene Hackman in his distinctive semi-transparent raincoat. And Murch is reminded of this by a story of Ondaatje's about W. H. Auden, who saw that a misprint in a proof produced a line better than his original: 'The poets know the name of the seas' became 'The ports know the name of the seas'. . . Oh, boy. If you're who I think you are, you would love *The Conversations*. Strangely, though, every friend I've pressed it upon so far has already read it, which suggests (*a*) that it's clearly one of those books whose reputation has grown and grown since it was first published, in 2002, and (*b*) my friends think I'm some kind of dimbo who only reads football reports and the lyrics of Black Sabbath songs.

And, in any case, it turns out that editing is kind of a metaphor for living. Our marriages, our careers, our domestic arrangements . . . so much of how we live consists of making meaning out of a bewildering jumble of images, of attempting to move as seamlessly as we can from one stage of life to the next.

There comes a time in the life of every young writer of fiction when he or she thinks, 'I'm not going to bother with plot and character and meaningless little slivers of human existence – I've done all that. I'm going to write about life itself.' And the results are always indigestible, sluggish and pretentious. If you're lucky, you get this stage over with before you're published – you have given yourself permission to rant on without the checks of narrative; if you're unlucky, it's your publisher who has given you enough rope with which to hang yourself, usually because your previous book was a brilliant success, and it can be the end of you.

Tinkers is Paul Harding's first novel, and it's pretty much about life itself, and it won him the Pulitzer Prize; he got away with it because he has a poet's eye and ear, and because he's a ruthless self-editor, and because he hasn't forgotten about his characters' toenails and kidneys even as he's writing about their immortal souls. (That's just an overexcited figure of speech, by the way, that bit about toenails and kidneys. There are no toenails in *Tinkers*, that I remember. I don't want to put anyone off.) Harding was at the Iowa Writers' Workshop, and I don't know whether he was taught by Marilynne Robinson, but if he was, then I would have loved to sit in on their tutorials; *Tinkers*, in its depth, wisdom, sadness and lightly worn mysticism, is reminiscent of Robinson's *Housekeeping*. (And I'm not suggesting for a moment he ripped her off, because you can't rip Marilynne Robinson off unless you, too, are wise and deep and possessed of a singular and inimitable consciousness.)

Tinkers is about a dying man called George Crosby; he's an old man, coming to the end of his natural life, and he's hallucinating and remembering, failing to prevent the past from leaking into the present. And George's dying is linked to his father, Howard's, life and eventual death. Howard sold household goods off the back of a wagon towards the beginning of the last century – he was a tinker. George repaired clocks. It's breathtakingly ambitious in its simplicity, but Harding is somehow able, in this novel that runs to less than 200 pages, to include the moments on which a life turns, properly imagined moments, moments grounded in the convincing reality of the characters. I was going to say that it's perhaps not the best book to take on holiday, because who wants to be reminded of his own mortality while he watches his children frolicking in the icy British surf? But then again, who wants to be reminded of his own mortality after he's wasted a day messing around on the internet instead of writing a very small section of a superfluous novel, or a screenplay that probably won't get turned into a film? On reflection, the holiday option is probably the better one: when my time comes, I hope that my children frolic before my eyes. I certainly don't want to see an unedited paragraph of a superfluous novel. ✶

NOVEMBER/DECEMBER 2010

Something has been happening to me recently – something which, I suspect, is likely to affect a significant and important part of the rest of my life. The grandiose way of describing this shift is to say that I have been slowly making my peace with antiquity; or, to express it in words that more accurately describe what's going on, I have discovered that some old shit isn't so bad.

Hitherto, my cultural blind spots have included the Romantic poets, every single bar of classical music ever written, and just about anything produced before the nineteenth century, with the exception of Shakespeare and a couple of the bloodier, and hence more Tarantinoesque, revenge tragedies. When I was young, I didn't want to listen to or read anything that reminded me of the brown and deeply depressing furniture in my grandmother's house. She didn't have many books, but those she did own were indeed brown:

cheap and old editions of a couple of Sir Walter Scott's novels, for example, and maybe a couple of hand-me-down books by somebody like Frances Hodgson Burnett. When I ran out of stuff to read during the holidays, I was pointed in the direction of her one bookcase, but I wanted bright Puffin paperbacks, not mildewed old hardbacks, which came to represent just about everything I wasn't interested in.

This unhelpful association, it seems to me, should have withered with time; instead, it has been allowed to flourish, unchecked. Don't you make yogurt by putting a spoonful of yogurt into something-or-other? Well, I created a half-century of belligerent prejudice with one spoonful of formative ennui. I soon found that I didn't want to read or listen to anything that anybody in any position of educational authority told me to. Chaucer was full of woodworm; Wordsworth was yellow and curling at the edges, whatever edition I was given. I read Graham Greene and John Fowles, Vonnegut and Tom Wolfe, Chandler and Nathanael West, Greil Marcus and Peter Guralnick, and I listened exclusively to popular music. Dickens crept in, eventually, because he was funny, unlike Sir Walter Scott and Shelley, who weren't. And because everything was seen through the prism of rock and roll, every now and again I would end up finding something I learned about through the pages of *New Musical Express*. When Mick Jagger happened to mention that 'Sympathy For The Devil' was inspired by Bulgakov's *The Master and Margarita*, off I trotted to the library. It didn't help that I was never allowed to study anything remotely contemporary until the last year of university: there was never any sense of that leading to this. If anything, my education gave me the opposite impression, of an end to cultural history round about the time that Forster wrote *A Passage to India*. The quickest way to kill all love for the classics, I can see now, is to tell young people that nothing else matters, because then all they can do is look at them in a museum of literature, through glass cases. Don't touch! And don't think for a moment that they want to live in the same world as you! And so a lot of adult life – if your hunger and curiosity haven't been squelched by your education – is learning to join up the dots that you didn't even know were there.

In some ways, my commitment to modernity stood me in good stead: those who cling to the cultural touchstones of an orthodox education are frequently smug, lazy and intellectually timid – after all, someone else has made all their cultural decisions for them. And in any case, if you decide to consume only art made in the twentieth century and the first part of the twenty-first, you're going to end up familiar with a lot of good stuff, enough to last you a lifetime. If your commitment to the canon means you've never had the time for Marilynne Robinson or Preston Sturges or Marvin Gaye, then I would argue that you're not as cultured as you think. (Well, not you. You know who Marvin Gaye is. But they're out there. They're out here, in Britain, especially.)

Over the last couple of years, though, I've been dipping into Keats's letters, listening obsessively to Saint-Saëns, seeking out paintings by Van Eyck, doing all sorts of things that I'd never have dreamed of doing even in my forties; what is even more remarkable, to me, at least, is that none of these things feel alien. There wasn't one single Damascene moment. Rather, there was a little cluster of smaller discoveries and awakenings, including:

1) Laura Cumming's magnificent book *A Face to the World: On Self-Portraits*, one of the cleverest, wisest books of criticism I've ever read. I wouldn't have picked it up in a million years if I hadn't known the author, and I ended up chasing after the self-portraits she writes about, which involved visiting galleries and old masters I'd carefully avoided until she taught me not to. (I read this book during my laughably unjust and

almost certainly illegal suspension from these pages last year, so I was unable to recommend it to you then, but you should read it.)

2) The Professor Green/Lily Allen song 'Just Be Good To Green'. I am old enough to remember not only the Beats International version, 'Dub Be Good To Me', but the SOS Band's original, 'Just Be Good To Me'. And I'm not saying that the Professor sent me off screaming towards Beethoven's late quartets (very good, by the way); I did, however, find myself wondering whether, when a song keeps coming round again and again and again, like a kid on a merry-go-round, there comes a point when you have to stop smiling and waving. Saint-Saëns is a new artist, as far as I'm concerned, with a big future ahead of him.

3) A new pair of headphones, expensive ones, which seemed to me to be demanding real food, orchestras and symphonies, rather than a wispy diet of singer-songwriter.

4) Jane Campion's beautiful film *Bright Star*, which turned Keats into a writer I recognized and understood.

5) During promotional work for *Lonely Avenue*, the project I've been working on with Ben Folds, the two of us were asked to trade tracks for some iTunes thing. Ben recommended an early Elton John album and the first movement of Rachmaninoff's Third Piano Concerto. I bought the Rachmaninoff, because the enthusiasm was so unaffected and unintimidating.

6) And now, Sarah Bakewell's biography of Montaigne, *How to Live*.

I had never read Montaigne before picking up Bakewell's book. I knew only that he was a sixteenth-century essayist, and that he had therefore wilfully chosen not to interest me. So I am at a loss to explain quite why I felt the need first to buy and then to devour *How to Live*. And it was a need, too. I have talked before in these pages about how sometimes your mind knows what it needs, just as your body knows when it's time for some iron, or some protein, or a drink that doesn't contain caffeine or absinthe. I suspect in this case the title helped immeasurably. This book is going to tell me how to live, while at the same time filling in all kinds of gaps in my knowledge? Sold.

Well, *How to Live* is a superb book: original, engaging, thorough, ambitious and wise. It's not just that it provides a handy guide to Hellenic philosophy, and an extremely readable account of the sixteenth-century French civil wars; you would, perhaps, expect some of that, given Montaigne's influences and his political involvement. (He became Mayor of Bordeaux, a city that had been punished for its insurrectionist tendencies.) Nor is it that it contains immediate and sympathetic portraits of several of Montaigne's relationships – with his wife, with his editor, and with his closest friend, La Boétie, who died in one of the frequent outbreaks of the plague, and of whom Montaigne said, famously, 'If you press me to tell why I loved him, I feel that this cannot be expressed, except by answering: Because it was he, because it was I.' The conventional virtues of a biography are all there, and in place, but where Bakewell really transcends the genre is in her organization of the material, and her refusal to keep Montaigne penned in his own time. In just over 300 pages, she provides a proper biography, one that takes into account the hundreds of years he has lived since his death; that, after all, is when a lot of the important stuff happens. And the post-mortem life of

Montaigne has been a rich one: he troubled Descartes and Pascal, got himself banned in France (until 1854), captivated and then disappointed the Romantics, inspired Nietzsche and Stefan Zweig, made this column possible.

He did this by inventing the medium of the personal essay, more or less single-handedly. How many other people can you think of who created an entire literary form? Indeed, how many people can you think of who created any cultural idiom? James Brown, maybe: before 'Papa's Got A Brand New Bag' there was no funk; and then, suddenly, there it was. Well, Montaigne was the James Brown of the 1580s. In his brilliant book *1599: A Year in the Life of William Shakespeare*, James Shapiro says that Montaigne took 'the unprecedented step of making himself his subject', thus enabling Shakespeare to produce a dramatic equivalent, the soliloquy. Of course, you can overstate the case for Montaigne's innovative genius. It's hard to imagine that, in the five-hundred-odd years since the essays were first published, some other narcissist wouldn't have had the idea of sticking himself into the middle of his prose. Montaigne invented the personal essay like someone invented the wheel. Why he's still read now is not because he was the first, but because he remains fresh, and his agonized agnosticism, his endearing fumbles in the dark (he frequently ends a thought or an opinion with a disarming, charming 'But I don't know'), become more relevant as we realize, with increasing certainty, that we don't have a clue about anything. I'd be surprised and delighted if I read a richer book in the next twelve months.

And then, as if Montaigne's hand were on my shoulder, I discovered Emily Fox Gordon's *Book of Days*, a collection of personal essays. I had read a nice review of them in the *Economist*, but had presumed that they'd be nicely written, light, amusing and disposable, but that's not it at all: these are not blogs wrapped up in a nice blue cover. (And is it OK, given the *Believer*'s no-snark rule, to say that some blogs are better than others? And that one or even two have no literary merit what-soever?) There are jokes in *Book of Days*, but the writing is precise, the thinking is complicated and original, and just about every subject she chooses – faculty wives, her relation-ship with Kafka, her niece's wedding – somehow enables her to pitch for something rich and important. If you are inter-ested in writing and marriage – and if you're not, then I don't know what you're doing round here, because I got nothing else, apart from kids and football – then she has things to say that I have never read elsewhere, and that I will be thinking about and possibly even rereading for some time to come. In Sarah Bakewell's introduction to *How to Live*, she quotes the English journalist Bernard Levin: 'I defy any reader of Mon-taigne not to put the book down at some point and say with incredulity, "How did he know all that about me?"' Well, I haven't yet had that experience with Montaigne – probably because, in my admittedly limited excursions so far, I've been looking for the smutty bits – but I felt it several times while I was reading *Book of Days*. 'The Prodigal Returns', the essay about Gordon's niece's wedding, turns into a brilliant medita-tion on the ethics and betrayals of memoir-writing, and contains the following:

What do I enjoy? Not staying in hotels, apparently. Not gluttony, not parties, not flattery, not multiple glasses of white wine. What I seem to want to do – 'enjoy' is the wrong word here – is not to have experiences but to think and tell about them. I'm always looking for excuses to avoid sitting down at my desk to write, but I 'enjoy' my life only to the extent that even as I'm living it, I'm also writing it in my mind.

Well. Obviously that's not me, in any way whatsoever. I'm an adventurer, a gourmand, a womanizer, a bon viveur, a surfer, a bungee jumper, a gambler, an occasional pugilist, a Scrabble player, a man who wrings every last drop from life's dripping sponge. But, you know. I thought it might chime with one or two of you lot. Nerds. And it certainly would have chimed with Montaigne.

I'm afraid I am going to recommend yet another epic poem about the Mau Mau uprising – this time Adam Foulds's extraordinary and pitch-perfect *The Broken Word*. It will occupy maybe an hour of your life, and you won't regret a single second of it. Foulds has written an apparently brilliant novel, *The Quickening Maze*, about the poet John Clare, in whom I have obviously had no previous interest, but this epic poem has the narrative drive of a novel, anyway. Set in the 1950s ('Der,' say the people who know all about the Mau Mau, which I'm presuming isn't every single one of you), it tells the story of Tom, a young Englishman who, in the summer between school and university, goes to visit his parents in Kenya and is drawn into a horrific, nightmarish suppression of a violent rebellion. If there were money to be made from cinematic adaptations of bloody, politically aware but deeply humanistic long-form poetry, then the film rights to *The Broken Word* would make Foulds rich.

Such is his talent that Foulds can elevate just about any banal domestic conversation. In the last section of the poem, Tom is attempting to seduce a young woman at university, and the dialogue is full of nos and that's not nices, the flat, commonplace rejections of a 1950s courtship. But what gives the passage its chilling power is everything that has gone before: how much of the violence Tom has seen is contained in him now? The control here is such that the language doesn't have to be anything other than humdrum to be powerful, layered, dense; and that's some trick to pull off. Why the Mau Mau uprising? At the end of the poem, Tom and the girl he has been forcing himself upon are looking in a jeweller's window; the children they would have had together, born at the end of the 1950s and early 1960s, sent to English public schools, are as we speak running our banks and our armies – our country, even.

These are three of the best books I've read in years, and I read them in the last four weeks, and they are all contemporary: *How to Live* and *Book of Days* were published in 2010, *The Broken Word* was published in 2008. So despite all my showing off and name-dropping, a narrative poem published two years ago and set in the 1950s is the closest I've come to the ancient world. But then, that's the whole point, isn't it? Great writing is going on all around us, always has done, always will. ✳

passengers struggling through some au courant literary monster, I have wanted to kiss you. I once gave a whole column over to *David Copperfield*, I remember, and more recently I raced through David Kynaston's brilliant but Rubenesque *Austerity Britain*. For the most part, though, there's a 'Stuff I've Been Reading'-induced, 500-page cut-off.

In the interests of full disclosure, I should add that I am a literary fattist anyway; I have had a resistance to the more amply proportioned book all my adult life, which is why the thesis I'm most likely to write is entitled 'The Shortest Book by Authors Who Usually Go Long'. *The Crying of Lot 49, Silas Marner, A Portrait of the Artist as a Young Man* . . . I've read 'em all. You can infer from that lot what I haven't read. And in any case, long, slow books can have a disastrous, demoralizing effect on your cultural life if you have young children and your reading time is short. You make only tiny inroads into the chunky white wastes every night before falling asleep, and before long you become convinced that it's not really worth reading again until your children are in reform school. My advice, as someone who has been an exhausted parent for seventeen years now, is to stick to the svelte novel – it's not as if this will lower the quality of your consumption, because you've still got a good couple of hundred top, top writers to choose from. Have you read everything by Graham Greene? Or Kurt Vonnegut? Anne Tyler, George Orwell, E. M. Forster, Carol Shields, Jane Austen, Muriel Spark, H. G. Wells, Ian McEwan? I can't think of a book much over 400 pages by any of them. I wouldn't say that you have to make an exception for Dickens, because we at the *Believer* don't think that you have to read anybody – we just think you have to read. It's just that short Dickens is atypical Dickens – *Hard Times*, for example, is long on angry satire, short on jokes – and Dickens, as John Carey said in his brilliant little critical study *The Violent Effigy: A Study of Dickens' Imagination*, is 'essentially a comic writer'. If you're going to read him at all, then choose a funny one. *Great Expectations* is under 600 pages, and one of the greatest novels ever written, so that's not a bad place to start.

Some months ago, I agreed to write an introduction to *Our Mutual Friend* – eight or nine hundred pages in paperback form, a terrifying two and a half thousand pages on the iPad – and I have been waiting for a gap in the *Believer*'s monthly schedule before attempting to embark on the long, long road. The recent double issue gave me an eight-week window of opportunity to read Dickens's last completed novel (only the unfinished *The Mystery of Edwin Drood* came after it) on top of something else, so I knew I couldn't put it off any longer.

I first read *Our Mutual Friend* years and years ago, and didn't enjoy the experience much, but I was almost certain that the fault was mine rather than the author's. Something was going on at the time – divorce, illness, a newborn, or one of the other humdrum hazards that turn reading into a chore – and *Our Mutual Friend* never really started to move in the way that the other big Dickens novels had previously done. (There's this moment you get a hundred or so pages in, if you're lucky and sympathetic to Dickens's narrative style and world view, when you feel the whole thing judder into life and pick up speed, like a train, or a liner, or some other vehicle whose size and weight make motion seem unlikely.) So I didn't worry about taking on the commission. I am in reasonable health, my next divorce is at least a year or so away, and I have given up having children, so I was sure that, this time around, I'd see that *Our Mutual Friend* is right up there with the other good ones – in other words, I was about to read one of the richest, most inventive, funniest, saddest, most energetic novels in literature.

Two-thirds of the way through, I was having such a hard time that I looked up a couple of contemporary reviews. Henry James thought it 'the poorest of Mr Dickens's works . . . poor with the poverty not of momentary embarrassment, but of permanent exhaustion'. Dickens's loyal friend John Forster admits that it 'will never rank with his higher efforts'. In other words, everyone knew it was a clunker except me – and even I knew, deep down, given that my first reading had been so arduous. And now, presumably, I have to write an introduction explaining why it's so great. What's great is the fifth chapter, an extended piece of comic writing that's as good as anything I've ever read by him. (If you have a copy lying about, start it and end it there, as if it were a Wodehouse short story.) What's not so great about it is not so easy to convey, because so much of it relates – yes – to length, to the plot's knotty overcomplications, stretched over hundreds and hundreds of pages. 'Although I have not been wanting in industry, I have been wanting in invention,' Dickens wrote to Forster sadly, after the first couple of parts had already been published in magazine form, and, as a summation of what's wrong with the book as a whole, that confession is hard to beat. It's interesting, I think, that nothing in *Our Mutual Friend* has wandered out of the pages of the novel and into our lives. There's no Artful Dodger, Uriah Heep, no Micawber, no Scrooge, no Gradgrind, no 'It was the best of times, it was the worst of times', no Miss Havisham, no Jarndyce v. Jarndyce. The closest we get is a minor character saying, apropos of another character's gift for storytelling, that 'he do the Police in different voices' – but Dickens needed a little help from T. S. Eliot for that particular stab at immortality. As far as I can tell, the novel has recovered from its poor reception, to the extent that it has become one of Dickens's most studied books, but that, I'm afraid, is no testament to its worth: it has endless themes and images and things to say about greed and poverty and money – in other words, endless material for essays – but none of that makes it any easier to get through. He'll be back in my life soon enough, but next time I might go for early Dickens, rather than late.

It now seems a very long time ago that I read Meg Wolitzer's forthcoming novel, *The Uncoupling*, and Colum McCann's National Book Award winner, *Let the Great World Spin*, and trying to think about them now is like trying to look over a very high wall into somebody's back garden. I know I enjoyed them, and they both seemed to slip by in a flash, but Dickens stomped his oversize boots all over them. I'm hoping that eventually they will spring back up in my mind, undamaged, like grass. McCann's novel, as many of you probably know, is set in New York City in August 1974, the summer that Philippe Petit walked between the Twin Towers on a tightrope. Underneath him, and all touched in some way by Petit's act of inspired insanity, lives McCann's cast of priests and lawyers, prostitutes and grieving mothers. It's a rich, warm, deeply felt and imagined book, destined, I think, to be loved for a long time. Regrettably, however, McCann makes a very small mistake relating to popular music towards the beginning, and so, as has happened so many times before, I spent way too long muttering at both the novel and the author. I must stress, once again – because this has come up before – that my inability to forgive negligible errors of this kind is a disfiguring disease, and I am determined to find a cure for it; I mention it here merely to explain why a book I liked a lot has not become a book that I have bought over and over again, to press on anybody who happens to be passing by. And it would be unforgivably small-minded to go into it . . . Ach. Donovan wasn't an Irish folk singer, OK? He was a Scottish hippie, and I hate myself.

Meg Wolitzer, like Tom Perrotta, is an author who makes you wonder why more people don't write perceptive, entertaining, unassuming novels about how and why ordinary people choose to make decisions about their lives. Take away the historical fiction, and the genre fiction, and the postmodern fiction, and the self-important attention-seeking fiction, and there really isn't an awful lot left; the recent success, on both sides of the Atlantic, of David Nicholls's lovely *One Day* demonstrates what an appetite there is for that rare combination of intelligence and recognizability. *The Uncoupling* is about what happens when all the couples in a New Jersey town stop having sex. (A magical wind, which springs up, not coincidentally, during rehearsals for a high-school production of Aristophanes' sex-strike comedy, *Lysistrata*, freezes the loins of all the post-pubescent women.) It's a novel that can't help but make you think about your own relationship – about what it consists of, what would be left if sex were taken away, how far you'd be prepared to go in order to keep it in your life somewhere, and so on. I have written all the answers to these questions down on a piece of paper, but I have locked the paper away in a drawer, and I'm not showing it to you lot. You know how much I get paid for this column? Not enough, that's how much.

The only thing I have read since Mr and Mrs John Harmon moved into Boffin the Golden Dustman's splendid house – that's an *Our Mutual Friend* spoiler, by the way, but I'm hoping I've spoiled it for you already – is Darin Strauss's *Half a Life*, a book that, as far as I'm concerned, could easily be republished under the title *The Opposite of Our Mutual Friend*. It's a short, simple piece of contemporary non-fiction, which in itself would be enough to make it look pretty good to me; it also happens to be precise, elegantly written, fresh, wise and very sad. Strauss was still in high school when he killed a girl in an accident: Celine Zilke, then aged sixteen, and a student at the same high school, inexplicably veered across two lanes before riding her bike right across his Oldsmobile. She died later, in the hospital. Strauss was completely exonerated by everybody concerned but, for obvious human reasons, the accident came to define him, and *Half a Life* is a riveting attempt to articulate the definition.

Any moral or ethical objection you might have to *Half a Life* – 'What right has he got to produce a book out of this when that poor girl was the victim?' – is dealt with very quickly, because, in part, *Half a Life* deals with the question of what right Strauss had to do anything at all. Was it OK to go back to school, laugh, go to the movies, look at anyone, feel sorry for himself, go to Celine's funeral, avoid her friends, talk to her parents, leave his bedroom? The author, a teenage boy, didn't have the answers to any of these questions, and they continued to elude him until well into adulthood. You could describe *Half a Life* as an elevated study of self-consciousness, in all senses of the compound noun – a book about a man watching his younger self watching his own every move, thought, feeling, checking and rechecking them before allowing them to escape into a place where they can be watched by other people – at which point the checking and rechecking start all over again. It's easy enough for us to say that what happened to Darin Strauss was a tragedy – not, of course, as big a tragedy as the one that befell Celine Zilke and her family, but a tragedy nonetheless. Easy enough for us to say, impossible for him to say – and therein lies Strauss's rich and meaningful material, material he works into a memorable essay. 'Whatever you do in your life, you have to do it twice as well now,' Celine Zilke's mother told him at the funeral. 'Because you are living it for two people.' Most of us can't live our lives well enough for one, but the care and thought that have gone into every line of *Half a Life* are indicative not only of a very talented writer, but of a proper human being.

And now Strauss has got me at it. I was going to end with a very good, if overcomplicated, joke about Dickens and a pair of broken Bose headphones, but I'm no longer sure it's appropriate. So I'll stop here. ✶

FEBRUARY 2011

It's a wet Sunday morning, and I'm sitting on a sofa reading a book. On one side of me is my eldest son, Danny, who is seventeen and autistic. His feet are in my lap, and he's watching a children's TV programme on his iPad. Or rather, he's watching a part of a children's TV programme, over and over again: a song from *Postman Pat* entitled 'Handyman Song'. Danny is wearing headphones, but I've just noticed that they're not connected properly, so I can hear every word of the song, anyway. On my other side is another son, my eight-year-old, Lowell. He's watching the Sunday morning football highlights programme *Goals on Sunday*. I'm caught between them, trying to finish Nicholson Baker's *The Anthologist*.

'Look at this, Dad,' Lowell says.

He wants me to watch Johan Elmander's goal for Bolton at Wolves, the second in a 3–2 win. It's one of the best goals of the season so far, and at the time of writing has a real chance of winning the BBC's Goal of the Month Award, but I only have thirteen pages of the novel to go, so I only glance up for a moment.

'Close the book,' Lowell says.

'I saw the goal. I'm not going to close the book.'

'Close the book. You didn't see the replay.'

He tries to grab the book out of my hand, so we wrestle for a moment while I turn the corner of the page down. I watch the replay. He's satisfied. I return to *The Anthologist*, football commentary in one ear and the *Postman Pat* song in the other.

Would Nicholson Baker mind? I'm pretty sure he wouldn't choose for me to be reading his work under these circumstances, and I'm with him all the way. I'd rather be somewhere else, too. I'd rather be on a sunlounger in southern California, in the middle of a necessarily childless reading tour, just for the thirty minutes it's going to take me to get to the end of the novel. I would savour every single minute of the rest of a wet English November Sunday with three sons, just so long as I was given half an hour – not even that! – of sunshine and solitude. I hope Baker would be pleased by my determination and absorption, though. I wasn't throwing his book away by submitting it to the twin assaults of *Postman Pat* and *Goals on Sunday*. I was hanging on to it for dear life.

It's a wonderful novel, I think, unusual, generous, educational, funny. The eponymous narrator, Paul Chowder, is a broke poet whose girlfriend has just left him; he's trying to write an introduction to an anthology of verse while simultaneously worrying about the rent and the history of rhyme. Chowder loves rhyme: he thinks that the blank verse of modernism was all a fascist plot, and that Swinburne was the greatest rhymer 'in the history of human literature'. Indeed, *The Anthologist* is full of artless, instructive digressions about all sorts of people (Swinburne, Vachel Lindsay, Louise Bogan) and all sorts of things (iambic pentameter) that I knew almost nothing about. Chowder might be an awful mess, but you trust him on all matters relating to poetry.

I developed something of a crush on Elizabeth Bishop after reading *The Anthologist*. I downloaded an MP3 of her reading 'The Fish', and on an overnight work trip to Barcelona I took with me a copy of Bishop's collected poems but no clean socks, which is exactly the sort of thing that Paul Chowder might have done. I would say that in my half-century on this planet so far, I have valued clean socks above poetry, so *The Anthologist* may literally have changed my life, and not in a good way. Luckily, it turns out that you can buy socks in Barcelona. Nice ones, too.

Pretty much everything I have read in the last month is related to the production of art and/or entertainment. Unlike all the others, Colm Tóibín's *Brooklyn* is not about art (and don't get sniffy about Céline Dion until I tell you what Carl Wilson has to say about her); it's about a young girl emigrating to the USA from a small town in Ireland in the 1950s. But as I am currently attempting to adapt *Brooklyn* for the cinema, it would be disingenuous to claim that the production of art and/or entertainment didn't cross my mind while I was re-reading it.

I haven't read a novel twice in six months for decades, and the experience was illuminating. It wasn't that I had misremembered anything, particularly, nor (I like to think) had I misunderstood much, first time around, but I had certainly forgotten the proximity of narrative events in relation to each other. Some things happened sooner than I was prepared for, and others much later – certainly much later than I can hope to get away with in a screenplay. You can do anything in a novel, provided the writing is good enough: you can introduce rounded, complex characters ten pages from the end, you can gloss over years in a paragraph. Film is a clumsier and more literal medium.

One thing that particularly struck me this time around is that though Tóibín's prose is precise and calm and controlled, *Brooklyn* is not an internal book. This is good news for a screenwriter, in most ways, but it did occur to me that if you strip away, as I have to do, all the control, then the story becomes alarmingly visceral. When Eilis travels third class on a ship to New York and ends up getting violently seasick and expelling her dinner through every available orifice . . . Well, if we show that onscreen, it will lose Tóibín's Jamesian poise. What you'll see, in fact, is a poor girl shitting copiously into a bucket. And Colm's devoted fans, aesthetes all, will say, 'Jesus, what has this hooligan done to our beautiful literary novel?' There might be art riots, in fact, similar to those that greeted *The Rite of Spring* when it was first performed, in 1913. People will throw stuff at me, and I'll be running out of the premiere shouting, 'There was diarrhoea in the book!' but nobody will believe me. I'm going to blame the director. Who made the *Porky's* movies? We should hire him.

The invention of the iPad means, as I'm sure you have discovered by now, that you can watch Preston Sturges movies pretty well anywhere you want. I have seen *Sullivan's Travels*, *The Lady Eve* and *The Palm Beach Story*, and though *Sullivan's Travels* remains my favourite, the minor characters in *The Palm Beach Story* are Dickensian in their weirdness and detail. It occurred to me that I know a lot more about, say, Montaigne and Richard Yates, having read very good books about them, than I do about Preston Sturges – a regrettable state of affairs, seeing as Sturges means more to me than either.

After reading Sarah Bakewell's brilliant *How to Live: A Life of Montaigne in One Question and Twenty Attempts at an Answer*, I came to understand how Montaigne invented soul-searching; after reading Blake Bailey's *A Tragic Honesty: The Life and Work of Richard Yates*, I saw why Yates's books are so incredibly miserable. Well, Donald Spoto's *Madcap: The Life of Preston Sturges* tells you everything you need to know about the pace of Sturges's movies: he lived that fast himself. He hung out with Isadora Duncan and Marcel Duchamp, took a job as assistant stage manager on Duncan's production of *Oedipus Rex*, travelled throughout Europe, ran branches of his mother's cosmetics company in New York and London, turned down a job as a one-hundred-dollar-a-week gigolo, and was honourably discharged from the US military. And then he turned twenty-one, and things got really interesting.

Sturges didn't really start writing until he was thirty; he began work on his first successful play, *Strictly Dishonorable*, on 14 June 1929, and finished it on 23 June. (According to his diary, he did no work on the fifteenth, sixteenth or twenty-second.) He received a telegram from a producer on 2 July suggesting an August production, and *Strictly Dishonorable* was one of the biggest Broadway hits of the 1930s. It made him a fortune. Even so, we here at the *Believer* recommend a ten- or fifteen-year gestation period for a first novel, play or screenplay: five years of writing, and then another five years of rewriting and editing. ('June 23: *Strictly Dishonorable* finished 5.40 this afternoon. Will polish tonight. Later: did so and drew set plans.') Yes, Sturges went on to write and direct *Sullivan's Travels*, and in 1947 was paid more than either William Randolph Hearst or Henry Ford II. But the slow, careful approach is unarguably more authentic and artistic, and will almost certainly result in a literary prize, or at least a nomination. (In defence of your creative-writing professors, Sturges did write a lot of stinkers for the stage. Robert Benchley, in the *New Yorker*, observed that 'the more young Mr Preston Sturges continues to write follow-ups to *Strictly Dishonorable*, the more we wonder who wrote *Strictly Dishonorable*'. You're not allowed to write cruel lines like that in this magazine, which is the only reason why I don't.)

I had no idea that Sturges's life had been so dizzyingly eventful; no idea, either, that he had changed the history of cinema by becoming the first Hollywood writer/director. He crashed and burned pretty spectacularly, too. He sank every dollar he had and a few hundred thousand more into a money pit of a club; and after a hot streak of seven good-to-great films between 1940 and 1944, it was effectively all over for him by 1949. He made only one more, apparently very bad, movie before he died, in 1959. Spoto's book can't help but zip along, although I did find myself skipping over the synopses of some of Sturges's Broadway farces. Farce, it seems to me, is curiously resistant to synopsis: 'He then makes his move to seduce Isabelle, but the judge enters, claiming it's his birthday and everyone must have champagne . . . The opera singer then re-enters with pyjamas for Isabelle . . . Gus puts pyjama top over her head, and as it slips down her teddy falls to the floor . . .' I am sure that, in 1930, *Strictly Dishonorable* was the hottest ticket in town, and that had I been alive to see it, I'd have promptly died laughing. But nothing, I fear, can bring the magic back to life now.

It is not stretching a point to say that the rapidly shifting sands of critical and popular approbation are the subject of Carl Wilson's brilliant extended essay about Céline Dion, *Let's Talk About Love: A Journey to the End of Taste*, another in the excellent 33⅓ series. Most of the others I've read (with the exception of Joe Pernice's novella inspired by The Smiths' *Meat Is Murder*) are well-written but conventional songs of praise to an important album in rock's history – *Harvest*, *Dusty in Memphis*, *Paul's Boutique*, and so on. This one is different. Wilson asks the question: why does everyone hate Céline Dion? Except, of course, it's not everyone, is it? She's sold more albums than just about anyone alive. Everyone loves Céline Dion, if you think about it. So actually, he asks the question: why do I and my friends and all rock critics and everyone likely to be reading this book and magazines like the *Believer* hate Céline Dion? And the answers he finds are profound, provocative and leave you wondering who the hell you actually are – especially if, like many of us around these parts, you set great store by cultural consumption as an indicator of both character and, let's face it, intelligence. We are cool people! We read Jonathan Franzen and we listen to Pavement, but we also love Mozart and *Seinfeld*! Hurrah for us! In a few short, devastating chapters, Wilson chops himself and all of us off at the knees. 'It's always other people following crowds, whereas my own taste reflects my specialness,' Wilson observes.

Let's Talk About Love belongs on your bookshelf next to John Carey's *What Good Are the Arts?* – they both cover similar ideas about the construct of taste, although Wilson finds more room for Elliott Smith and the Ramones than Professor Carey could. And in a way, taking on Dion is a purer and more revealing exercise than taking on some of the shibboleths of literary culture, as Carey did. After all, there is a rough-and-ready agreement on literary competence, on who can string a sentence together and who can't, that complicates any wholesale rejection of critical values in literature. In popular music, though, a whole different set of judgements is at play. We forgive people who can't sing or construct a song or play their instruments, as long as they are cool, or subversive, or deviant; we do not dismiss Dion because she's incompetent. Indeed, her competence may well be a problem, because it means she excludes nobody, apart from us, and those who invest heavily in cultural capital don't like art that can't exclude: it's confusing, and it doesn't help us to meet attractive people of the opposite sex who think the same way we do.

Wilson's book isn't just important; it has good facts in it, too. Did you know that in Jamaica, Céline is loved most of all by the badasses? 'So much that it became a cue to me to walk, run or drive faster if I was ever in a neighbourhood I didn't know and heard Céline Dion,' a Jamaican music critic tells Wilson. And did you know that the whole highbrow/middlebrow thing came from nineteenth-century phrenology, and has racist connotations? Why aren't I surprised?

I may well have to insist that you read this book before we continue our monthly conversation, because we really need to be on the same page. My own sense of self has been shaken, and from this moment on, there may be only chaotic enthusiasm (or sociological neutrality) where there was once sensible and occasionally inspired recommendation. I may go and have a look at that Elmander goal again. It might help to ground me. You can still have good goals and bad goals, right? Right? *

MARCH/APRIL 2011

BOOKS BOUGHT:
* ★ *The Immortal Life of Henrietta Lacks* – Rebecca Skloot
* ★ *The Last Englishman: The Double Life of Arthur Ransome* – Roland Chambers

BOOKS READ:
* ★ *Game Change: Obama and the Clintons, McCain and Palin, and the Race of a Lifetime* – John Heilemann and Mark Halperin
* ★ *The Immortal Life of Henrietta Lacks* – Rebecca Skloot

In April 2010, I was a tragic victim of the volcanic ash cloud that grounded all flights into, out of and across Europe for a few days. I am sure that other people have hard-luck stories, too: weddings, births and funerals were missed, job opportunities went begging, feckless husbands given one last chance got home to find their underwear strewn across the street, and so on. Mine, however, was perhaps more poignant than any of them: my family, stranded in Tenerife, was unable to celebrate my fifty-third birthday with me. Can you imagine? Of all the birthdays to miss, it had to be the one I was looking forward to the most. All my life I had wondered what it would be like to turn fifty-three, to open presents suitable for a fifty-three-year-old – something from the excellent Bald Guyz[1] range

---

[1] Bald Guyz makes head wipes, moisturizing gel and all kinds of great stuff for men who have chosen to live a hair-free life. The company has not paid for this endorsement, but I am very much hoping it will, or that it will send me a crate of free stuff.

of beauty products, for example, or a Bruce Springsteen box set – while an adoring family looked on. Well, my adoring family was stranded on an island in the Mediterranean, in a hotel that apparently laid on a chocolate fountain for breakfast. When they eventually made it home, my birthday was clearly an event to be celebrated when it came around again in 2011, rather than retrospectively. I have therefore decided, perhaps understandably, that this April I will be turning fifty-three again. It's not a vanity thing; it's simply that I'm owed a birthday.

Back in 2010, I had to make do with the cards I'd been dealt, and the cards were these: a small group of friends bought me champagne, which we drank in my garden on a beautiful spring evening, at a time when I would usually be embarking on some terrible, strength-sapping, pointless fight about, say, shampoo and/or bedtime; the same friends then took me to a favourite local restaurant and gave me presents. You can see why I might feel bitter even to this day.

Three of the presents my friends had bought me were book-shaped; and, miraculously, given the lack of deferred gratification in my book-buying life, I wanted to read them all and didn't own any of them. I got a lovely first edition of Mordecai Richler's *The Apprenticeship of Duddy Kravitz*, a copy of *Game Change: Obama and the Clintons, McCain and Palin, and the Race of a Lifetime* by John Heilemann and Mark Halperin, and Marc Norman's history of screenwriting, *What Happens Next*. Is it too late and too hurtful to say that my fifty-third birthday was perhaps the best ever?

Several months later, and I have finally read one of the three, even though I wanted to read all three of them immediately. (What happened in between? Other books, is what happened. Other books, other moods, other obligations, other appetites, other reading journeys.) *Game Change*, as you may or may not know, is about the 2008 election in the USA, and appeared in a couple of the best-of-year lists here in the UK, so I was reminded that I owned it; when I read it, I was reminded that politicians are unlike anyone I have ever met in my life.

Maybe some of you know politicians. Maybe you hang out with them, went to school with them, exchange Christmas cards with them. I'm guessing not, though. Politicians tend not to hang out with people like you, almost by definition. Typically, someone interested enough in the arts to be reading the *Believer* has spent a lot of time doing things that disqualify you not only from a career in politics, but from even knowing people who have a career in politics. While you were smoking weed, sleeping around, listening to Pavement, reading novels, watching old movies and generally pissing away every educational opportunity ever given to you, they were knocking on doors, joining societies, reading the *Economist*, and being very, very careful about avoiding people and situations that might embarrass them later. They are the people who were knocking on your door five minutes after you arrived at college, asking for your vote in the forthcoming student-representative election; you thought they were creeps, and laughed at them behind their backs. Meanwhile, they thought you were unserious and unfocused, and patronized you irritatingly if you ever had cause to be in the same room. I hope that, however old you are, you have already done enough to kill any serious political ambition. If you haven't wasted huge chunks of your life on art, booze and soft drugs, then you've wasted huge chunks of your life, and we don't want you around here. Go away.

Many of the characters in *Game Change* are quite clearly creeps. They are not portrayed as creeps, for the most part. John Heilemann and Mark Halperin obviously like the people who want to govern us, and their book, which is an unavoidable, enthralling mix of the gossipy and the profoundly significant, reflects this affection. And yet I defy anyone from around these parts to read this book

without thinking, over and over again, 'Who are these people?'
There's John Edwards, of course, whose affair with the extraordinary Rielle Hunter was conducted more or less entirely in full view
of an increasingly incredulous staff; when Edwards eventually realized the damage he had done to himself and his campaign, he
lambasted a young staffer because he didn't come to his boss 'like a
fucking man and tell me to stop fucking her'. But there are plenty
of other strange people, too – people who don't really seem to
believe anything, but who are desperately anxious to know what the
country wants to hear them saying.

Obama is different, of course, but it's still very difficult to fathom
why anyone would want to become a world leader. It's really not a
nice job. For $400,000 a year, plus an entertainment budget of
$19,000 – although I would imagine very little of that can go on
CDs, books and cinema tickets – you give up safety, family life,
social life, sleep, a significant proportion of your sanity and the
esteem of approximately two in every three of your fellow citizens.
I am not being flippant: this is an intolerable prospect, for anyone
with any sense of an inner life. This means that the people who
want to represent us are actually the least representative people in
the world.

Here in Europe, we still love Obama. But right at the beginning
of *Game Change*, when Halperin and Heilemann are describing his
relationship with Hillary Clinton, there is a line intended to convey
how close the two were, once upon a time, but that serves only to
make you wonder about politicians as a species: 'At one point,
Obama gave her a gift: a photograph of him, Michelle, and their
two young daughters, Sasha and Malia.' So, hold on . . . Hillary was
Barack's mother? Because if she wasn't, why on earth would he give
her a picture of himself and his kids? Would you do that with someone you knew professionally? 'Here's a framed picture of me. Put it
up anywhere in your house. It doesn't have to be on your mantel-

piece. Or put it up in your office, on the half a shelf you have available for photos of your loved ones.' Try it, and see how often you're invited to after-work drinks.

Game Change isn't the book I thought it would be, perhaps because the nomination race and the presidential campaign were not what they looked like from across the Atlantic. I was expecting a thrilling and inspirational story, full of goodies and baddies, dizzying highs and dispiriting lows; instead, Heilemann and Halperin describe a long, strength-sapping and bitter trudge to victory. Much of the book is taken up with the inevitability of Clinton's defeat, and her refusal to acknowledge it, while Obama waits with weary impatience. And the fight between Obama and McCain is a non-event once Sarah Palin joins in and makes the sides uneven. This is not to say that *Game Change* is dull. It isn't, because every page feels like the truth. It's just that the truth isn't as uplifting as you want to believe.

It was the holiday season here in the UK, which explains the brevity of the 'Books Read' list: my intellectual life is utterly dependent on my children attending school. The holiday season doesn't explain why I didn't pick up any fiction, nor does it explain why I should choose to spend all my available reading time on the unpromising subjects of American politics and cancer cells. I will only regret it if *Game Change* and *The Immortal Life of Henrietta Lacks* turn out to be the last two books I ever read, because I don't think they illustrate the breathtaking range of my literary tastes. They make me look like the kind of non-fiction guy I meet on planes during book tours. 'Should I have heard of you? See, I don't read many novels. I like to learn something I didn't know already.' At the time of writing I am halfway through a short and very beautiful YA novel, the completion of which should recomplicate me; meanwhile, you'll have to forgive these pages of the *Believer* temporarily resembling the books section of *Business Traveller* magazine.

Maybe the business travellers know what they're talking about, though, because *The Immortal Life of Henrietta Lacks* is riveting, beautifully written and, yes, educational. I learned stuff. I learned so much stuff that I kept blurting it out to anyone who'd listen. Do you know who Henrietta Lacks was? Have you ever heard of the HeLa cells? Did you know that they can be found in just about any research lab in the world? And so on. I'll tell you, you don't want to be living with me at the moment. I'm even more boring than usual.

Rebecca Skloot's extraordinary book is the story of a dirt-poor black woman who died an agonizing death from cervical cancer in 1951. Just before Henrietta died, however, a surgeon sliced off a piece of her tumour and gave it to a research scientist called George Gey, who had been trying to grow human cells for years. Henrietta's cells, however, grew like kudzu, for reasons that are still not entirely clear to scientists; they grew so fast, so uncontrollably, that when you look up HeLa on Wikipedia, the entry uses the word 'contamination' in the first four lines. HeLa is so powerful and fierce and durable, so eager to reproduce itself, that it gets into everything.

After I had read the first three or four chapters, I was a little worried on Skloot's behalf: I thought she was telling the story too quickly. Henrietta's cells were duplicating, her place in medical history was assured . . . maybe the last couple of hundred pages would turn out to be the first one hundred rehashed and analysed, and the book would lose its breathtaking opening momentum. But the author knows what she has, and what she has is a goldmine of material dealing with class, race, family, science and the law in America. In fact, *The Immortal Life of Henrietta Lacks*, like Adrian Nicole LeBlanc's incredible *Random Family*, is about pretty much everything. (*Random Family* and Skloot's book both took a decade to research and write, perhaps not coincidentally. I suspect that, in both cases, the subject matter grew richer and richer with each year of contemplation.) Skloot tells brief, vivid and astonishing stories of medical-ethics cases; she follows the cells as they get blasted into space and help find a vaccine for polio; she weaves in the lives of Henrietta's children as they struggle through the decades following their mother's death. They had no idea that she had achieved immortality until the 1970s, because nobody had ever taken the trouble to tell them, or to ask their permission – a courtesy denied Henrietta herself, of course. And while you can go online this very second and buy HeLa cells, the Lacks family has struggled, mostly in vain, for employment, access to health care and recognition for Henrietta's contribution to science. If I come across a book as good, as gripping, as well constructed and as surprising as this in the rest of 2011, I will be a happy and grateful man.

Contemporary fiction is OK, but you don't really learn anything from it, do you? It's mostly written by a bunch of arty losers who couldn't be bothered to go out and get a proper job, and who don't know anything about the world, anyway. Non-fiction, that's the thing. Or historical fiction, because you know when you're reading it that people have done a whole load of research into nineteenth-century brick-making. Or thrillers, because you can learn a lot of things about high-grade weaponry. My New Year's resolution is to get a job as a, you know, a business guy, and join a business-guy book club. Plus, I'm going to befriend an important politician, a minister or a secretary of state. If any of you ministers or secretaries of state out there subscribe to this magazine and read this column, then Facebook me, OK? I am literally holding my breath, so hurry. ✻

MAY 2011

I first and last read John Updike when I was in my twenties: I devoured all the *Rabbit* books that had been published at that point, and looked forward to a time in my life when I would be old enough to understand them. All that adultery and misery and ambition and guilt looked completely thrilling back then – but mystifying, too. Where did it all come from? And why, aged twenty-five, was I not grown up enough to be experiencing any of it? What was wrong with me? I suspect I didn't read any more of Updike's novels after that point simply because they made me feel inadequate, in ways that

I hadn't previously considered. New forms of inadequacy I could live without, seeing as I didn't know what to do with the ones I was already aware of.

I'm not quite sure why an unread copy of *Marry Me* winked at me from my bookshelves just before I flew to the USA for a work trip recently. On the cover of the book, Paul Theroux promises us that 'Updike has never written better of the woe that is marriage', but I can assure you (and my wife) that it wasn't the cheery blurb that lured me in. Perhaps I wanted to test myself again, a quarter of a century after the last time: had I got any closer to adulthood? Would I now, finally, be able to see a reflection of my own domestic circumstances?

> 'You dumb cunt,' he said, and bounced her into the mattress again and again, 'you get a fucking grip on yourself. You got what you wanted, didn't you? This is it. Married bliss.'
>
> She spat in his face, ptuh, like a cat, a jump ahead of thought; saliva sprayed back down upon her own face and as it were awakened her . . .

I am embarrassed to say that life is only very rarely like this chez nous. There's the holiday season, obviously, and the occasional Saturday night, especially during January and May, when, typically, my football team Arsenal crash out of the major competitions. But, hand on heart, I could not claim that we scale these particular giddy heights of seriousness with the kind of frequency that would allow me to gasp with recognition. I was even more cowed by the way this scene concludes, half a page and fourteen lines of dialogue later:

> 'You're a nice man.' She hugged him, having suppressed a declaration of love.
>
> Wary, he wanted to sleep. 'Good night, sweetie.'

I don't like to point the finger, and in any case my wife is generally a pacific and forgiving person. But the truth is that whenever I do call her the c-word and bounce her into the mattress again and again, she has never once told me that I'm 'a nice man' – she tends to remain cross with me for hours. This means, in turn, that I have never been able to find it in myself to say, 'Good night, sweetie,' and put the whole unfortunate episode behind us. In other words, it's her fault that we are not yet Updikean. She's a 45-year-old child.

It wasn't just the rows I found hard to comprehend; some of the sex was beyond me, too:

> Though Sally had been married ten years, and furthermore had had lovers before Jerry, her lovemaking was wonderfully virginal, simple, and quick.

Ah, yes. That's what we gentlemen want: women who are both sexually experienced and alive to the touch, while at the same time not too, you know, trampy. 'Wonderfully virginal'? My therapist would have more fun in fifty minutes than he'd ever had in his whole professional life were I to use that particular combination of adverb and adjective in a session.

Marry Me was, as you can probably imagine, totally compelling, if extraordinarily dispiriting in its conviction that trying to extract the misery out of monogamy is like trying to extract grapes from wine. We worry a lot about how technology will date fiction; it had previously occurred to me that books written in the last quarter of the twentieth century would lead me to wonder whether something fundamental has changed in the relationships between men and women. I'm not sure we do feel that husbands and wives are doomed to suspicion, enmity and contempt any longer, do we? Or am I making a twit of myself again? I suppose it's the latter. It usually is.

Worryingly – and this must remain completely between us – I recognized myself more frequently in the checklist Jon Ronson refers to in the title of his book than I did in *Marry Me*. (I'm not going to repeat the title. You'll have to go to the trouble of glancing back at the 'Books Road' list, and maybe you won't bother, and then you'll think better of me.) 'Glibness/superficial charm'? Well, I have my moments, even if I do say so myself. And have you lost some weight? 'Lack of realistic long-term goals'? I wouldn't call literary immortality unrealistic, exactly. It's more or less happened to Chaucer and Shakespeare, and I'm miles better than either of those. 'Grandiose sense of self-worth'? Ah, now there at least I can plead not guilty. 'Need for stimulation/proneness to boredom'? I literally stopped in the middle of typing out that last sentence in order to play Plants v. Zombies, although I did get bored of that after a couple of hours, so perhaps there is hope for me. 'Poor behavioural controls'? Again, there is a glimmer of light, because I have just put out my last cigarette and eaten my last biscuit.

Jon Ronson, as those of you who have read *Them* or *The Men Who Stare at Goats* will know, is a fearless non-fiction writer, so familiar with, and curious about, the deranged and the fanatical that he probably asks for his hair to be cut with a lunatic fringe. *Them* dealt with extremists of all hues, and *The Men Who Stare at Goats* was about that section of the American military who believe that one day wars might be won using mind-control and gloop. *The Psychopath Test*, as the title suggests, cuts straight to the chase.

It begins with a mystery: why were a group of academics, mostly neurologists, all sent a book by 'Joe K' that consisted entirely of cryptic messages and holes? The perplexed neurologists believed that Ronson was the man to solve the puzzle, and their instincts were sound, because he does so. On the way, he meets a man who pretended to be mad in order to escape a prison sentence, and now cannot convince anybody that he is sane; several Scientologists engaged in a war on psychiatry, as Scientologists tend to be; Bob Hare, the man who devised the eponymous test; and a top CEO whose legendary ruthlessness leads Ronson to suspect that he might tick a few too many boxes. (It is Bob Hare's contention that psychopaths are all around us, in positions that allow them to exert and abuse their authority.) Like all Ronson's work, *The Psychopath Test* is funny, frightening and provocative: it had never occurred to me, for example, that Scientologists had any kind of an argument for their apparently absurd war on science, but Ronson's account of the equally absurd experiments and treatments for which respected psychiatrists are responsible gives one pause for thought.

If you are a subscriber to this magazine, and a regular reader of this column, and you have very little going on in your life, and you're kind of anal, you may be thinking to yourself, 'Hey! It's eight weeks since he last wrote a column, and he's read exactly four books!' There are various explanations and excuses I could give you, but the two most pertinent are as follows:

1) I have been cruelly tricked into co-founding a writing centre for kids, with a weird shop at the front of it, here in London (and don't even think about copying this idea in the USA unless you want to hear from our lawyers – although why you would want to spend a thousand hours and a million pounds a week doing so I can't imagine).

2) I have spent way too much time watching the Dillon Panthers, the fictional football team at the heart of the brilliant drama series *Friday Night Lights*. (And yes, I know, I know – I have seen the fourth season. I am being respectful to those who are catching up.)

Reading time, in other words, has been in short supply, even during the day, and half the reading that has got done is directly related to the above. H. G. Bissinger's terrific non-fiction book, the source for a movie and then the TV series, is about the Permian Panthers, who represent a high school in Odessa, Texas, and regularly play in front of crowds of 20,000 – or did, when the book was published in the early 1990s. There is no equivalent of high-school or college football in Europe, for several reasons: there are no comparable sports scholarships, for a start, and, in a country the size of England, it's quite hard to live more than fifty miles from a pro team. And in any case, because your major sports have turned out to be so uninteresting to the rest of the world, young talent in the USA is governable; the young soccer players of London and Manchester no longer compete solely with each other for a place in a top professional team, but with kids from Africa and Asia and Spain. Over the last several years, Arsenal have routinely played without a single English player in their starting eleven. Our best player is Spanish; one of our brightest hopes for the future is Japanese and currently on loan to a club in Holland. So the idea of an entire community's aspirations being embodied in local teenage athletes is weird, but not unappealing.

The reality, as Bissinger presents it – and he went to live in Odessa for a year, hung out with players and coaching staff and fans, so he knows what he's talking about – is a lot darker, however. It turns out that there are not as many liberals in small-town Texas as the TV series would have me believe: in Dillon, people are always speaking out against racism, or talking about art, or thinking about great literature. (The adorably nerdy Landry Clarke can quite clearly be seen reading *High Fidelity*, my first novel, in an episode of the third season. This is almost certainly the greatest achievement of my writing career. And I'm sorry to bring it up, but I had to tell somebody.) In Odessa, Dillon's real-life counterpart . . . not so much

racism gets confronted, or towering masterpieces of fiction consumed. Bissinger loves his football, and falls in love with the team,
but is powerfully good on what the town's obsession with football
costs its kids. It's not just the ones who don't make it, or become
damaged along the way, all of whom get chucked away like ribs
stripped of their meat (and catastrophically uneducated before
they've been rejected); the kids who can't play football are almost
worthless. The girls spend half their time cheerleading and
cake-baking for the players, and the students with more cerebral
interests are ignored. In the season that Bissinger followed the team,
the cost of rush-delivered post-game videotapes that enabled the
coaches to analyse what had gone right and wrong was $6,400. The
budget for the entire English department was $5,040. And the team
used private jets for away games on more than one occasion. Isn't it
great how little you need to spend to inculcate a passion for the arts?
Perhaps I have drawn the wrong conclusion.

David Almond's *My Name Is Mina* is an extraordinary children's
book by the author of *Skellig*, one of the best novels written for
anyone published in the last fifteen years. And this new book is
a companion piece to *Skellig*, a kind of prequel about the girl
who lives next door. It's also, as it turns out, a handbook for anyone who is interested in literacy and education as they have been,
or are being, applied to them or their children or anybody else's
children:

> Why should I write something so that somebody could say I was
> well below average, below average, average, above average, or well
> above average? What's average? And what about the ones that find
> out they're well below average? What's the point of that and how's
> that going to make them feel for the rest of their lives? And did Wil-
> liam Blake do writing tasks just because somebody else told him to?
> And what Level would he have got anyway?

'Little Lamb, Who mad'st thee?
Dost thou know who mad'st thee?'
What level is that?

Almond's wry disdain for the way we sift our children as if they were potatoes killed me, because I was once found to be below average, across the board, at a crucial early stage in my educational career, and I have just about recovered enough confidence to declare that this judgement was, if not wrong, then at least not worth making. I think that, like everybody, I'm above average at some things and well below at others.

My Name Is Mina is a literary novel for kids, a Blakean mystic's view of the world, a fun-filled activity book for a rainy day ('EXTRA-ORDINARY ACTIVITY – Write a poem that repeats a word and repeats a word and repeats a word and repeats a word until it almost loses its meaning'), a study of loneliness and grief, and it made more sense to me than half the fiction I usually read. This can't be right, and I won't allow it to be right. For literary purposes only, I am off to call my wife obscenities and bounce her up and down on a mattress. As I write, she's upstairs, helping my youngest son with his homework, so she's in for a shock. ✷

JUNE 2011

My friendship with the writer Sarah Vowell – history buff, TV and radio personality, occasional animated character – is now fifteen years old. For the first decade or so, it was pretty straightforward: whenever I was in New York, we would sit in a park staring at a statue of an obscure but allegedly important American figure, and she would talk about it while I nodded and smoked. Over the last few years, however, it has become complicated to the extent that it has started to resemble one of those Greek myths where the hero (in this case, me) is asked to perform tasks by some enigmatic and implacable goddess (her) or monster (also her). Vowell isn't as well known in the UK as she should be – we have different chat shows, for a start, and because of the awesomely uncompromising insularity of her writing, her books aren't published here. So, as one of her few English fans, I have been taking the literary challenges that she throws across the Atlantic personally. In my mind, at least, it goes like this. I tell her that I am an enormous admirer of her work, and she says, 'In that case, I am going to write a book about the mu-seums of the assassinated American Presidents, excluding the most recent, and therefore the only one you are interested in. Will you read it?'

I read it, loved it, told her so.

'I see that you are a worthy English opponent, so I will have to try harder. I will now make you read a book about New England Puritans – not the Plymouth Pilgrims, but the more obscure (and more self-denying) Massachusetts Bay crowd.'

I read it, loved it, asked her to hit me with something a little less accessible.

And now she has come roaring back with *Unfamiliar Fishes*, a history of Hawaii, although obviously it's not a complete history of Hawaii, because a complete history of Hawaii would not have intimidated the English reader to quite the required extent, and might have contained some fun facts about Bette Midler. Vowell wisely chose to concentrate on the nineteenth century, post 1820, when her old friends from New England sailed around the entire American continent in order to tell the natives that everything they had hitherto believed was wrong. (One of the many things I had never thought about before reading *Unfamiliar Fishes* was the sheer uselessness of New England as a home base for missionaries. It took them a good six months to get to anywhere uncivilized enough to need them.)

Unfamiliar Fishes tells the story of the battle for hearts and minds between the Massachusetts killjoys and the locals. In these wars, the liberal conscience always has us rooting for the locals, even though we invariably already know that we are doomed to disappointment, and that the locals, whoever and wherever they might be, are even as we speak tucking into Happy Meals, listening to Adele, and working for Halliburton. In Hawaii, though, there was a lot invested in the idea that a child born from the union between brother and sister was superior to a child conceived any other way, and this particular belief kind of muddied the water a little for me. I know, I know. Different times, different cultures. But I have a sister, and you too may well have a sibling who operates an entirely different genital system. And if you do, then you might find yourself unable to boo the meddling Christians with the volume you can usually achieve in situations like this.

And yet, as Vowell points out, the whole foundation of royalty is based on the notion that one bloodline is superior to another, and therefore shouldn't be messed with:

> The way said contamination is prevented is through inbreeding, which, of course, is often the genetic cause of a royal dynasty's demise through sterility, miscarriages, stillbirths, and sickliness. That would be true of the heirs of Keopuolani just as it was true of the House of Hapsburg.

In other words, one of the reasons that my own country is in such a mess is that there simply hasn't been enough inbreeding: if there had, we might be shot of our Royal Family by now. Incest is more complicated than it looks (and please feel free to go and get that printed on a T-shirt, if it's a slogan that grabs you). Like anything else, it's got its good points and its bad.

The one team we can all get behind in *Unfamiliar Fishes* is the

crew of the English whaler *John Palmer*. They were so annoyed by
the missionaries messing with their inalienable right to onboard visits from prostitutes that they started shelling the port. I am, however,
grudgingly respectful of the Americans who, convinced of the
Hawaiians' need for a Bible, first helped to invent a written Hawai-
ian language, and then translated the whole thing from the original
Greek and Hebrew. It took them seventeen years. Finally, I have a
notion of what I might do when I retire. Anyway, I have sailed
through yet another task set by the dark nerd-maiden from across
the water; I don't think she is capable of writing anything that I
wouldn't read, although I hope she doesn't take that as a provoca-
tion. And her history of whaling on the island was so enthralling
that it got me through the entire first chapter of *Moby-Dick*.

The idea of this column, for those of you who have arrived eight
years late, is that I write about what I have read in the previous
month; for some reason, the books I read with my children have
never been included. This last couple of months, however, we have
been reading Andy Stanton's *Mr Gum* series at bedtime, and as Stanton's books are providing as much joy to me as they do to the boys,
their omission from these pages would be indefensible.

Mr Gum is an evil, joyless, smelly old man who tries to poison
dogs, and whose favourite TV programme is *Bag of Sticks*, which is
as exciting as it sounds. His best friend is the evil butcher Billy William the Third, and his enemies are the entirely admirable Polly,
Friday O'Leary and the billionaire gingerbread man with electric
muscles, little Alan Taylor. The books are a happy product of a tol-
erably non-incestuous relationship between Roald Dahl and Monty
Python, and they are properly funny: Stanton has an eccentric
imagination and an anarchic verbal wit that occasionally redirects
his narrative in directions that possibly even the author didn't expect.

My sons' enormous enjoyment of the books has been intensified
through a series of superb readings by their father, readings that, in

his mind at least, are comparable only to the performances Dickens is reported to have given at public events. Billy William the Third is rendered as an evil version of the great English comic actor Kenneth Williams, Alan Taylor as the football commentator John Motson, and Mr Gum as a kind of ancient Cockney gangster paterfamilias. It seems ridiculous that performances with this level of invention take place night after night in a child's bedroom, in front of an audience of two; I may well have to throw them open to the public.

If you, like me, have been cursed by boy children, you too may have found that their relationship with books is a fractious one, no matter how many times they see a male role model lounging around the house with his nose glued to a partial history of Hawaii. Andy Stanton's series has been a real breakthrough, and a testament to the importance and the power of jokes; we are just about to start the seventh of the eight books, and I'm already fearful of the Gumless future.

I don't have the heart to tell my sons that the older one gets, the less funny literature becomes – and they would refuse to believe me if I tried to explain that some people don't think jokes even belong in proper books. I won't bother breaking the news that, if they remain readers, they will insist on depressing themselves for about a decade of their lives, in a concerted search for gravitas through literature. Charles Portis is a *Believer* favourite (one of our editors wrote an enormous and completely excellent piece about him in the very early days of this magazine's life) partly because he takes his humour seriously: the Coen Brothers' recent adaptation of *True Grit* was admirable in many ways, but it didn't really convey the comic brilliance of the novel, nor was it able to, as so much of it was embedded in the voice of the priggish, God-fearing Mattie Ross. I suspect that we have the Coen Brothers to thank for the reappearance of Portis's first novel, *Norwood*, in bookstores, so they have done their bit for comedy, anyway.

'Norwood' is Norwood Pratt, a marine who obtains a hardship discharge so that he can return to Texas to look after his incapable sister Vernell. Vernell promptly marries an unlikeable disabled veteran called Bill Bird, however, thus liberating Norwood to go to New York, partly in an attempt to reclaim seventy dollars that an army friend owes him. So *Norwood* is a road-trip book, and the simplicity of its structure allows for a dazzling range of eccentric minor characters and plenty of room for any number of terrific, short, often crazily pointless passages of dialogue. Here's Norwood, on a bus, trying to engage with a two-year-old called Hershel Remley:

> 'I believe the cat has got that boy's tongue,' said Norwood.
>
> 'Say no he ain't,' said Mrs Remley. 'Say I can talk aplenty when I want to, Mr Man.'
>
> 'Tell me what your name is,' said Norwood. 'What is your name?'
>
> 'Say Hershel. Say Hershel Remley is my name.'
>
> 'How old are you, Hershel? Tell me how old you are.'
>
> 'Say I'm two years old.'
>
> 'Hold up this many fingers,' said Norwood.
>
> 'He don't know about that,' said Mrs Remley. 'But he can blow out a match.'

There's so much to love here: the portrayal of the clearly slow-witted toddler, Mrs Remley's desperate and hopeful pride, the author's merciless ear for disastrous parental anthropomorphizing . . . This is the third novel I have read by Charles Portis, and I am now completely convinced that he's a neglected comic genius. And here's a cool fact: in Nora Ephron's new book of essays, *I Remember Nothing*, she talks about dating Portis in the 1960s. The relationship clearly didn't last, but it feels as though their children are everywhere, anyway.

Tom Rachman's *The Imperfectionists*, which I suspect you may have read already, is an ingeniously structured work of fiction that manages to tell the entire history of an English-language newspaper based in Rome through a series of linked short stories about its members of staff. This, to me, makes *The Imperfectionists* a collection rather than a novel, despite the bald assertion on the cover ('A Novel'), and I slightly resented being misled, for entirely indefensible reasons; in most ways I haven't aged at all over the last quarter of a century, remarkably, but I seem to have developed some kind of old-geezerish resentment of story collections. Is that possible? Is resentment of short fiction a sign of ageing, like liver spots? And if it is, then why? As the end of one's life draws closer, surely one should embrace short fiction, not spurn it. And yet I was extremely conscious of not wanting to make the emotional effort at the beginning of each chapter, to the extent that I could almost hear myself grumbling like my grandmother used to. 'Who are these people, now? I don't know them. Where did the other ones go? They'd only just got here.' It's a great tribute to Rachman, to his sense of pace and his choice of narrative moment, that within a couple of pages I had forgiven him. And the world of the expatriate is, it occurred to me halfway through the book, rich with fictional possibilities; almost by definition, the characters are lost, restless, discontented – just the way we like them.

I feel that I cannot leave before explaining some of the more baffling choices in the 'Books Bought' column. Lawrence W. Levine's *Highbrow/Lowbrow* was, along with John Seabrook's *Nobrow*, a recommendation from a reader who felt it might help me with some of the difficult issues raised by Carl Wilson's essay on Céline Dion; the book about Ronald Reagan's time at General Electric I bought after watching a riveting Reagan documentary on the BBC. The chances of me reading either of them are, I suspect, slim; as is so often the case, however, I am, at relatively modest expense, intent on maintaining a risible self-delusion about my intellectual curiosity. I know way too much about James Brown already, so I'll probably choose that one next. ✶

JULY/AUGUST 2011

No time spent with a book is ever entirely wasted, even if the experience is not a happy one: there's always something to be learned. It's just that, every now and again, you can hit a patch of reading that makes you feel as if you're pootling about. There's nothing like a couple of sleepy novels, followed by a moderately engaging biography of a minor cultural figure, to make you aware of your own mortality. But what can you do about it? We don't choose to waste our reading time; it just happens. The books let us down.

It wasn't just that I enjoyed all the books I read this month; they felt vital, too. If you must read a biography of a sitcom star, then make sure the sitcom is the most successful and influential in TV history.

You have a yen to read about a grotesquely dysfunctional communist society? Well, don't mess about with Cuba – go straight for North Korea. John Lanchester's *Whoops!* is a relatively simple explanation of the biggest financial crisis in history; Mark Twain's *Adventures of Huckleberry Finn* is, according to Hemingway, the book from which all American literature derives. A month of superlatives, in other words – the best, the worst, the biggest and the most important.

And, as a digestif, David Eagleman's *Sum*, which invites us to contemplate forty varieties of afterlife. It's such a complete package that it seems crazy to carry on reading, so I may well stop altogether. I'm not giving this column up, though. It pays too well.

Stefan Kanfer's *Ball of Fire* contains an anecdote which seems to me to justify not only the time I spent reading it, but the entire genre, every biography ever written. Kanfer is describing the early days of Ball's relationship with Desi Arnaz, which was stormy right from the off:

> Almost every Sunday night ended with a furious argument about each other's intentions and infidelities . . . It happened that two of the town's greatest magpies witnessed many of the quarrels. F. Scott Fitzgerald and his inamorata, columnist Sheilah Graham, used to watch the spats from Fitzgerald's balcony.

F. Scott Fitzgerald used to watch Lucille Ball and Desi Arnaz fighting? Why didn't I know this before? If this story is true – and there's no reason to doubt it – then all is chaos. No biography can be left unread, just in case there is a gem like this lying there, undiscovered, within its pages. Maybe Thomas Pynchon repeatedly bangs on Sarah Michelle Gellar's wall because she plays her music too loud! Maybe Simon Cowell and Maya Angelou are in the same book group!

The reason Kanfer's book works so well, and why it throws up so many good stories, is that Ball, like the fictional Mose Sharp and Rocky Carter in Elizabeth McCracken's brilliant *Niagara Falls All Over Again*, took the long road through the American pop-culture century. She worked in theatre, film, radio and TV. She dated Henry Fonda, worked with the Marx Brothers, knew Damon Runyon. A washed-up Buster Keaton helped her with her physical comedy. She found out that she was pregnant by listening to Walter Winchell on the radio – he'd obtained the information from the lab technicians even before they passed the information on to Ball's doctor. She attracted the attention of HUAC, the House Un-American Activities Committee, because she'd registered with the Communist Party in 1936 primarily to humour her socialist grandfather. Hers was an extraordinary journey, and just in case you need a little more, there was a long, tempestuous marriage at the centre of it. (Ball rendered the first divorce from Arnaz null and void by jumping into bed with her ex-husband on the way back from the courthouse.) We didn't have a Lucille Ball in the UK; you have way more female comediennes than us. This is not a coincidence.

There wasn't any logic behind my decision to go straight from *Ball of Fire* to the banking crisis, although John Lanchester's *Whoops!* (published in the USA as *I.O.U.*) certainly bolstered the sense of elegiac melancholy that lingers after you've said goodbye to Lucy and Desi and the Golden Age of Television. We now have more to worry about than the end of wholesome, nation-uniting family sitcoms; it turns out that the Golden Age of Everything is over. One of Lanchester's contentions is that:

> Western liberal democracies are the best societies that have ever existed . . . Citizens of those societies are, on aggregate, the most fortunate people who have ever lived.

I'll be comparing and contrasting with North Korea a little later, but when you consider that one of the indicators of poverty in the USA and the UK is obesity, you can see his point. Nobody is obese in North Korea.

Now, however, the citizens of the USA and the UK have some bills to pay. One authoritative market commentator puts the cost of the bailout in the USA at just over $4.5 trillion – a number:

> . . . bigger than the Marshall Plan, the Louisiana Purchase, the Apollo moon landings, the 1980s savings and loan crisis, the Korean War, the New Deal, the invasion of Iraq, the Vietnam War, and the total cost of NASA's space flights, all added together – repeat, added together (and yes, the old figures are adjusted upward for inflation).

If you were thinking of knocking on the door of a government body because you're looking for a little help with your video installation . . . well, I'd give it a few weeks. Here in the UK, the government is looking to make an unprecedented and almost certainly unachievable 25 per cent cut in public services; we need to find in the region of £40 billion a year simply to service our debts.

There are plenty of numbers in *Whoops!* Most of them are scary, but some are funny, if your taste in humour leans towards the apocalyptic. In a brilliant chapter about the catastrophic failure of the mathematical models of risk used by bankers and economists, a chapter entitled 'The Mistake', Lanchester introduces us – well, me, anyway – to the notion of the sigma, a measure of probability:

> A '3-sigma event' is something supposed to happen only 0.3 per cent of the time, i.e., about once every three thousand times something is measured.

According to the mathematical models, the 1987 Black Monday crash was a 10-sigma event; this means that, were the life of the universe repeated 1 billion times, it still shouldn't have happened. And yet it did. During the recent crash, the CFO of Goldman Sachs claimed that he was seeing twenty-five-sigma events *'several days in a row'*. (My italics, but I'm sure I'm italicizing for all of us.) Lanchester tries to give us some sense of the numbers involved here, but it's basically hopeless:

> Twenty sigma is ten times the number of all the particles in the known universe; 25-sigma is the same but with the decimal point moved fifty-two places to the right.

Even if we presume that there are three particles in the known universe – and I'm no physicist, but I'm guessing that three is probably on the low side – then the number is still impossible to grasp. And these people saw events on this scale of incomprehensible improbability happening every day for a week. They would presumably also have been staggered by Brazil winning the next World Cup, on the basis that they didn't win it yesterday or the day before or on any of the four and a half thousand days since their last victory, in 2002. (For those of you who don't follow soccer: Brazil are quite good. They always have a decent chance of winning the World Cup. But the World Cup takes place only every four years, so . . . Oh, forget it.) Meanwhile, the reality underpinning the numbers and the credit swaps and the securitization was a whole bunch of people who had been persuaded to take out mortgages that they couldn't afford, and had to pay more for them than people with a credit history and a job, because they were riskier. One thing that had never quite sunk in for me is that, for Wall Street and the City, subprime mortgages and junk bonds are Good Things – or used to be, anyway – so it wasn't as though the unscrupulous were hiding shoddy goods under the more attractive stuff. The shoddy goods were attractive, and they wanted in. The higher the risk, the more money you make. Lovely. And the bankers thought they'd fixed it so that this risk had no downside, ever, for anyone. Securitization and its trimmings were, almost literally, alchemy, as far as the banks could tell.

One of the reasons *Whoops!* has done well in the UK is that John Lanchester is One of Us. He's not a financial journalist; he's a novelist, and a critic, and an outsider when it comes to this stuff. His dad was a bank manager, though, and he has the necessary interest, and the necessary anxiety. I watched *Inside Job* this month, too, and between them, Lanchester and Charles Ferguson have achieved the impossible, and made me feel . . . not knowledgeable, exactly, but at least I can see the dim light of comprehension breaking somewhere over the horizon. I don't know you personally, but I'm sort of presuming that you know more about The Decemberists and Jennifer Egan than you do about Gaussian copula formulas. Is that right? If so, then this is the book for you.

Nothing to Envy is a book about what happens when an economy fails completely, to the extent that there is nothing left – no work, no infrastructure, no food, no anything. I bought it after a forceful recommendation from a friend, and after it won a non-fiction prize in the UK, and I wasn't sure I'd ever read it. But on the very first page there is a startling satellite picture of the Korean peninsula, taken at night, and I was hooked in. In this picture, the South looks like the USA or the UK or just about any twenty-first-century country, mottled with light from its cities, and great puddles of the stuff in the area around Seoul. In the North, it looks as though someone has a single candle burning in the capital, Pyongyang. Much of North Korea has no electricity. It's packed up. It went sometime in the early 1990s, and it never came back. Sometimes – typically on the birthday of the Great Leader – it wheezes back into life for an hour or two, but the rest of the time North Korea is lost in a blackness of its own making.

Barbara Demick has pieced together a picture of daily life in this poor benighted country from the testimonies of people who got out. They weren't dissidents, because dissidence doesn't really exist in North Korea. How can it, when its citizens have never been presented with an alternative way of thinking, and when they have no access to books, magazines, newspapers, movies, TV, music or ideas from any other part of the world? Even conversation is dangerous, when you have no way of knowing whether your friends, neighbours, even children are informants. You don't have a telephone, and you can't write to anyone when you have no pen or paper, and even if you do, the postman may well burn your letters simply because there's nothing else to burn. Meanwhile, everyone is starving to death. (Much of the book is about life in the 1990s but, as Demick's epilogue and the most cursory Google search makes clear, nothing much has changed.) One of Demick's interviewees was a kindergarten teacher who saw her class go from fifty to fifteen kids. There is literally nothing to eat; they're peeling the bark off trees and boiling it up for soup. This is a country whose inhabitants have literally shrunk, while the rest of the world has got taller: the average North Korean seventeen-year-old boy is five inches smaller than his counterpart in the South.

A review quoted on my paperback edition tells us that this book is 'required reading for anyone interested in the Korean peninsula'; I've just spent a few hundred words telling you how harrowing much of it is. We're not selling it to you, I can tell. And yet *Nothing to Envy* does have resonance, and it does transcend its subject matter, if that's what you want it to do. Both *Whoops!* and *Nothing to Envy* make it clear just how utterly dependent we all are on systems; without them, our much-cherished quirky individuality and our sense of moral self mean nothing. And I know this sounds weird and possibly callous, but Demick's book was every bit as absorbing as *Ball of Fire*: both contain a multitude of extraordinary stories,

SEPTEMBER 2011

I know that you are younger than me, because more or less every-one is, nowadays. I am presuming, too, that if you have turned to this page of the *Believer* then you have an interest in books, and that if you read any of the rest of the magazine, then you are likely to have a deep passion for other forms of art. It is not too much of a stretch, then, to deduce from this information that your sexual relationships are complicated, morally dubious and almost certainly unsavoury, and I say that with as much neutrality as I can muster. So before I write about *Mating in Captivity*, Esther Perel's book about monogamous sex, I suppose I should clarify a couple of points for you.

Firstly: monogamy is this thing where you sleep with only one person. And I'm not talking about only one person during the whole length of Bonnaroo, or an art-film screening, or a poetry 'happening', or whatever. Sometimes the commitment might last weeks, months even. (Married readers: in next month's column, I may introduce some more information, although I suspect they're some years away from being able to handle the dismal truth.) Esther Perel has cleverly recognized that a tiny minority of monogamists can occasionally feel a twinge of inexplicable and indefinable dissatisfaction with their chosen path – nothing significant, and certainly nothing that leads them to rethink their decision (monogamous relationships almost never fail, unless either partner is still sexually active) – and she has written a book that might help them through this tricky time. It's a niche market, obviously, the sexual equivalent of a guide for people whose pets have an alcohol-abuse problem. It's great that someone has done it, but it's not for everyone.

Secondly, I should also explain that I read this book for professional reasons, and professional reasons alone: I'm trying to write something about monogamy, God help me. I know that sounds dubious, but maybe you will believe me if I confess that my own marital problems lie beyond the reach of any self-help book available in a bookstore, or even on Amazon. They also lie beyond the reach of pills and tears, but perhaps I have said too much.

Mating in Captivity is a very wise book – I was going to say 'surprisingly wise', because I have hitherto maintained the lit-snob assumption that non-fiction books that purport to improve your unhappy marriage or your failing career or your sickly spiritual well-being will actually do no such thing. (As we know around these parts, only Great Literature can save your soul, which is why all English professors are morally unimpeachable human beings, completely free from vanity, envy, sloth, lust, and so on.) Perel is very good on how the space between couples in which eroticism thrives, a space we are desperate to fill in the early days of a relationship, can be shrunk by domesticity and knowledge; there is a pragmatic understanding in her writing that is entirely winning and sympathetic.

She also has interesting things to say about the contemporary insistence that all intimacy is verbal intimacy, a cultural diktat that confuses and intimidates the kind of male whose inability to talk is then misinterpreted as an inability to commit, or a macho fear of weakness. Perel tells the rather sweet story of Eddie and Noriko, who literally couldn't communicate because they didn't speak the same language; Eddie had been ditched by scores of women who were impatient with his apparent unwillingness to bare his soul. 'I really think that not being able to talk made this whole thing possible,' Eddie tells Perel, twelve years into his marriage:

'For once, there was no pressure on me to share. And so Noriko and I had to show how much we liked each other in other ways. We cooked for each other a lot, gave each other baths . . . It's not like we didn't communicate; we just didn't talk.'

More baths, less talking . . . If you're a woman who is currently and unhappily single, you could do a lot worse than put that slogan on a banner and march up and down your street.

'Some of America's best features – the belief in democracy, equality, consensus-building, compromise, fairness, and mutual tolerance – can, when carried too punctiliously into the bedroom, result in very boring sex,' Perel says in a chapter entitled 'Democracy Versus Hot Sex'. At the time of writing, Michele Bachmann has just announced her candidacy for the presidency, and another assumption I have made about you is that very few of you vote Republican. I don't think Esther Perel is encouraging you to do so, although if the unthinkable happens and Bachmann wins, there may well be some consolations, from the sound of it. (None of this applies to the British, of course, who live in a class-ridden monarchy, and as a consequence have hot sex every single day of their lives.)

My only complaint about this engaging and thoughtful book is that its author uses the word 'vanilla' pejoratively too often, as a synonym for bland, dull, safe. This usage, I think, must stem from vanilla ice cream, which, typically, tastes of nothing and is certainly the unthinkable option if you're in an ice-cream establishment that offers scores of varieties. The flavour of the vanilla pod itself, however, is sophisticated, seductive, subtle. Have you tried the Body Shop Vanilla Shower Gel? I don't want to write advertising copy for multinational companies – not for free, anyway – but Body Shop Vanilla, it seems to me, is much more suggestive of deviance and light bondage than it is of the missionary position. And, guys, if you use that, could you credit the *Believer*? And also chuck them a few quid? Thanks.

I bought a couple of the books on the lists above after coming across a top five that Woody Allen put together for the *Guardian*. I had never heard of Machado de Assis, and I probably wouldn't have thought of reading a biography of Elia Kazan had it not been for Allen's recommendation, but Richard Schickel's book chimed with the mood created by *Ball of Fire*, Stefan Kanfer's terrifically entertaining book about Lucille Ball, which I read recently.

Kazan, as you may or may not know, was the brilliant director of *On the Waterfront* and *A Streetcar Named Desire*. But he is now remembered almost as clearly because he chose to testify against former colleagues in front of the House Un-American Activities Committee (HUAC), in 1952. Schickel begins his book, electrifyingly and provocatively, by coming out swinging on Kazan's behalf. I had never come across anyone attempting to do this before, and as a consequence I had always presumed that those who named names could safely be written off. God knows there are few enough examples of moral choices that are straightforwardly good or bad, and I had always valued the decision of Kazan and others as one of those that one didn't have to think about: they were wrong, full stop, and we are thus free to condemn them as viciously and as cheerfully as we want.

Yes, well. It turns out that it wasn't quite like that. Schickel's arguments are complicated and detailed, and I don't have the space to do them justice here, but then, complication and detail are precisely what have been lacking ever since the 1950s. Schickel describes the campaign against Kazan as 'a typical Stalinist tactic – seize the high, easy-to-understand moral ground, then try to crush nuanced opposition to that position through simplifying sloganeering'. I suspect that I'm not the only one who liked the look of that easy-to-understand moral ground, and there is a part of me that is actually irritated to discover that it's not as comfortable as it appeared. Schickel's jabs at the kidney – if that is where our fuzzy sense of morality is stored – are telling and sharp: naming names would have been fine if the names named had belonged to the Ku Klux Klan or the Nazi Party; there were lots of other, more democratic leftist organizations that liberals could have signed up for; there were public protests against the Gulags as early as 1931, and there was really no excuse for those who defended Stalin in the 1950s; much of the outrage directed against Kazan was entirely synthetic. Rod Steiger, who appeared in *On the Waterfront* and was loudly and angrily opposed to the idea of Kazan receiving an honorary Oscar in 1999, told a reporter from *Time* that Kazan 'was our father and he fucked us'; Schickel points out that the fucking was done well over a year before *On the Waterfront* started shooting – in other words, Steiger's moral objections came to the surface painfully slowly, and well after one of the most celebrated performances of his film career was safely in the can.

It was Dalton Trumbo, one of the writers blacklisted as a result of HUAC, who ended up making the best case for Kazan. The kind of person who testified, he said, was:

> . . . a man who has left the CP to avoid constant attempts to meddle with the ideological content of his writing . . . a person whose disagreement with the CP had turned to forthright hostility and who, when the crunch came, saw no reason to sacrifice his career in defence of the rights of people he now hated . . .

All I want is one simple article of faith that is even less complicated than it looks. Is that too much to ask?

There is a lot more to Kazan than all this, of course. He directed the first production of *Death of a Salesman*, as well as the stage version of *A Streetcar Named Desire*, worked with Arthur Miller on several other occasions, slept with Monroe and Vivien Leigh, made *East of Eden* and wrote a novel that sold four million copies in the USA – Kazan had a pretty impressive twentieth century. I wish Schickel's book had been just that little bit more gossipy, not just because gossip is fun, but because Kazan's relentless womanizing, it seems to me, needed some kind of explanation or context. Schickel's refusal to discuss Kazan's domestic arrangements seems indulgent, rather than high-minded; Kazan is given a guys-will-be-guys (or, perhaps, great-artists-will-be-great-artists) free pass that I don't think anyone ever really earns. From the index: 'Kazan, Molly Day Thacher (first wife) husband's affairs and, 94–95, 388–89, 404.' They were married for thirty years.

Philip Roth was recently quoted as saying that he doesn't read fiction any more. 'I wised up,' he told an interviewer in the *Financial Times*. We all have moments like this: I have vowed, at various points, never to read any more novels, and books about sport, and thrillers where kids get murdered, and music biographies; but none of these decisions ever holds for very long. Moods change, tastes reassert themselves, and a great book always shakes off its genre and its subject matter, anyway – although I fear that the desire to read about the dismemberment of children and young women may have left me for ever. I'm not sure wisdom has much to do with any of this, and I'd hate for Roth's words to be given extra weight just because of his age, his accomplishments and the veneration he inspires. I don't know if it's ever very wise to give up on Dickens. In my experience, a sudden panic about my own ignorance is followed firstly by the desperate desire to read non-fiction, and then, usually very swiftly, by a realization that any non-fiction reading I do is going to be hopelessly inadequate and partial. If I knew I was going to die next week, then I'd definitely be keen to read up on facts about the afterlife; in the absence of any really authoritative books on this subject, however (no recommendations, please), then I think I'd rather read great fiction, something that shoots for and maybe even hits the moon, than a history of the House of Bourbon.

It is, perhaps, a little unfair to ask Eleanor Henderson to provide a philosophical justification for an entire art form, especially as *Ten Thousand Saints* is her first novel, but she does a pretty good job, anyway. She moves in extraordinarily close to her young protagonists, participants in the New York straight-edge punk scene of the 1980s, and in doing so taught me a lot of things I didn't know. (Straight-edge was never much of a thing in England, where sobriety is seen as a moral failing by all ages and tribes.) The big draw here, though, is Henderson's writing, which is warm, engaged and precise; I don't think I have ever come across a gritty urban novel that is as uninterested in finding a prose style to complement its subject. That's a good thing, by the way. *Ten Thousand Saints* is the

OCTOBER 2011

BOOKS BOUGHT:

* *Stone Arabia* – Dana Spiotta
* *Kings of Infinite Space* – James Hynes
* *The Waterfall* – Margaret Drabble
* *To Live Outside the Law: Caught by Operation Julie, Britain's Biggest Drugs Bust* – Leaf Fielding

BOOKS READ:

* *Hellhound on His Trail: The Stalking of Martin Luther King, Jr and the International Hunt for His Assassin* – Hampton Sides
* *The Fear Index* – Robert Harris
* *Next* – James Hynes
* *The Anti-Romantic Child: A Story of Unexpected Joy* – Priscilla Gilman

It is August and, as I write, burned-out buildings in London and other British cities are being demolished after several nights of astonishing and disturbing lawlessness. Meanwhile I am in the Dorset village of Burton Bradstock, listening to the sound of the wind-whipped sea smashing on to the shore, and to the young daughter of a friend playing 'Chopsticks' over and over and over again on the piano belonging to the cliff-top house we have rented. It's unlikely that the riots would have made it into these pages at all had it not been for *Hellhound on His Trail*, Hampton Sides's book about the murder of Martin Luther King Jr and the hunt for his assassin, James Earl Ray. Just as Tottenham and Hackney, just a couple of miles from my home, were being set alight, I was reading about the same thing happening in Washington DC on the night of 5 April 1968, twenty-four hours after Ray shot King while he was standing on the balcony of the Lorraine Motel in Memphis. There were 500 fires set in DC that night; the pilot who flew Attorney General Ramsey Clark back to the capital from Memphis thought that what he saw beneath him looked like Dresden. And here in Burton Bradstock it became impossible not to compare London in 2011 with DC in 1968. It wasn't an instructive or helpful comparison, of course, because it could only induce nostalgia for a time when arson seemed like the best and only way to articulate a righteous and impotent fury. And while it is true that a violent death sparked our troubles (a black man named Mark Duggan was shot and killed by police), it was not easy to see the outrage in the faces of the delirious white kids helping themselves to electronic goods and grotesquely expensive sneakers. Luckily for us, every single politician, columnist, leader writer, talk-show host and letters-page contributor in Britain knows why all this happened, so we should be OK.

Hellhound on His Trail is a gripping, authoritative and depressing book about a time when, you could argue, it was much easier to talk with confidence about cause and effect. James Earl Ray, King's assassin, was a big supporter of segregationist George Wallace and his independent push for the White House; Ray also liked the look of Ian Smith's reviled apartheid regime in Rhodesia. He was eventually arrested at Heathrow as he attempted to make his way to somewhere in Africa that would let him shoot black people without all the fuss that he had caused in the USA. Sides has little doubt that he acted alone, and indeed one of the lowering things about his book is the reminder, if one needed it, that it takes very little to kill a man; you certainly don't need the covert cooperation of the CIA or the FBI or the KKK. You just need enough money to buy a decent hunting rifle.

Of course, there are lots of people who have a vested interest in persuading us that the recent past is easier to read than the present.

Paul Greengrass, the director of *Green Zone* and *United 93*, has for some time been wanting to make a film about the last days of MLK, but this year the project collapsed, apparently because the guardians of the King estate objected to depictions of King's extramarital affairs in the script. 'I thought it was fiction,' said Andrew Young, who was with King on the night he died. And yet King's womanizing was, according to Sides, both real and prodigious; he spent the night before he died in room 201 of the Lorraine Motel with one of his mistresses, the then Senator of Kentucky, Georgia Davis. Davis has even written a book, *I Shared the Dream*, about her relationship with King. I haven't read Greengrass's script, but it looks as though Andrew Young is attempting, four decades after Memphis, to sanctify his friend in a way that can only impede understanding. Jesse Jackson, meanwhile, attempted to impede understanding there and then: he told TV interviewers that he was with King on the balcony (he wasn't) and, according to Sides, smeared his shirt with King's blood before appearing on TV chat shows. The trouble with history, it seems to me, is that there are too many people involved. The next time something historical happens, someone should thin out the cast list. Oh, and by the way, did you know that James Earl Ray was arrested in London, by detectives from Scotland Yard? Oh, yes. Your guys had done some handy groundwork, though, we'll give you that much.

It has, it must be said, been something of a gloomy reading month, not least because my brother-in-law has written another novel. *The Fear Index* is his fifth since I started writing this column, back in 2003. I have managed only three in the same period, and though I have also managed to squeeze out a screenplay for a movie, so has he. As I write, he is lying by a swimming pool in the South of France, whereas I am looking through a window at the grey English Channel. I am looking through a window (*a*) because if I ventured outside I would be blown into the grey English Channel by the gale that is currently blowing, and (b) because I have a column to write, and therein, I think, we find the root cause of my brother-in-law's superior output and income. 'Stuff I've Been Reading' is now well over 100,000 words long, and if I could somehow take those words back and rearrange them into a stylish, ingenious, compelling and intelligent contemporary thriller, then I would. But there you are. My commitment to your literary health is such that I'm prepared to let my children shiver in their little wetsuits, although I don't suppose you're the remotest bit grateful. I wish I could tell you that *The Fear Index* is a resounding failure that will lie in unsold heaps all over Europe and the USA, but I can't. Actually, why can't I? It's my column, and there are very few other advantages to writing it, as I have very recently realized. *The Fear Index* is a resounding failure that will lie in unsold heaps all over Europe and the USA. I'm not going to tell you what it's about. You'll only want to buy it.

I suppose it wouldn't be giving too much away to tell you that *The Fear Index* is a financial-crisis thriller, the second book about the terrifying instability of our banking system that I've read in the last couple of months. The other was John Lanchester's brilliant *Whoops!*, in which Lanchester says that, 'Western liberal democracies are the best societies that have ever existed . . . Citizens of those societies are, on aggregate, the most fortunate people who have ever lived.' There isn't much downside to being the luckiest people in history, but in James Hynes's brilliant novel *Next*, which I read because the editors of this magazine gave it a prize, Hynes's protagonist, Kevin Quinn, is fiftyish and struggling – struggling, at least, with all the things there are to struggle with in prosperous contemporary America. His career has been nudged, gently and undramatically, into a backwater; he has a relationship with a younger woman he doesn't love. He spends most of his time – or most of the eight or nine hours covered in the novel, anyway – daydreaming about a couple of the standout sexual experiences of his life.

Quinn is travelling from Ann Arbor to Austin for a job interview, on a day when there have been major terrorist attacks in Europe. He's uncomfortable flying, as we all are in those periods, but this doesn't stop him mooning over the young, sexy Asian girl sitting next to him on the flight, and when he bumps into her again in Austin, he ends up killing the time before his appointment by trailing idly after her, in an aimless and unthreatening kind of a way. He gets very hot, and extremely lost, both in Austin and in his own underwhelming and regret-filled past. It's all very real and very familiar, at least to this fifty-plus male.

Hynes writes with the sort of knowing, culturally precise, motor-mouthed internal chatter that brings to mind David Gates's two monumental novels, *Jernigan* and *Preston Falls*, and I can think of no greater recommendation: Hynes and Gates populate their books with men I recognize. They're not the intimidatingly brainy and, to me, alienating creatures you find in Great American Novels by Great American Novelists. There's less rage, more doubt, more regret – and, in the case of Kevin Quinn, more of a sense that he is entirely the author of his own misfortune. His failure can't be pinned on an event or on a scheming, ball-busting woman. Rather, it's due to too much introspection, distraction, indiscipline. Quinn hasn't worked hard enough at anything.

And *Next* takes a dizzying, heartbreaking, apocalyptic and oddly redemptive turn. As it turns out, the atrocities are not confined to small European countries far away. As Kevin is, finally, on his way to his interview, the cab driver is listening on the radio to news of attacks much closer to home, in Minnesota, where he has a brother. The cabbie is nervous, distracted, upset; he makes frantic phone calls. Kevin, though, is oblivious to all of this. He's recreating, in pornographic detail, a night he spent a long time ago with a girl called Lynda. 'You need to pay attention, man,' the cabbie tells him, devastatingly, at the end of his ride, but it's too late for Kevin.

Violent deaths take place in all three of the books described above – in fact, I can't recall a more distressing reading month. And most of the fatalities are deeply upsetting, rather than fun, although in *The Fear Index* my brother-in-law does get to bump off a sleaze-bag we don't like very much. So I needed the respite of Priscilla Gilman's *The Anti-Romantic Child*, which, though serious, contains no bloodshed, and is all the better for it. A memoir about raising a child with special needs would not have been improved by scenes of indiscriminate slaughter. (This is the sort of quality advice you'll be getting when you enrol in my online writing school, coming soon.)

As regular readers of this column may have noticed, I don't read many first-person books on this subject, despite, or almost certainly as a direct result of, being the father of a disabled child myself. There are many reasons for this, and I have a feeling I've droned through some of them before, so I'll give it a rest this time around. However, I would like to observe that it's hard to find books in this genre with ideas in them, and that's where *The Anti-Romantic Child* scores. It's not just about dealing with the tricky hand that the author has been dealt; this is also a book about literature, specifically Wordsworth and the Romantics, and how Gilman's literary heroes (she used to teach their work) have both helped and hindered her understanding of what her child is and what she wanted him to be. It's smart, soulful and involving, and it rang plenty of bells for me; I also ended up reading more Wordsworth than I have ever done in my entire life. I understand the appeal a little more than I did, but I would still argue that there is more in those poems about the natural world than is strictly necessary.

I haven't read as much in Dorset as I wanted to. Perhaps that is what happens when you invite thirty-five kids to share your holiday home with you. (I wish that number were satirical in some way, but it's not.) I have, however, discovered a new product, the Waboba ball, which bounces off water and is completely tremendous. I'm not sure I can make a case for its literary qualities, which may mean that it has no place in this magazine. But those of us who contribute to the *Believer* have found that we have enormous influence over the manufacturers of leisure products, and that whenever we mention one we are bombarded with offers of free samples, exotic trips to Caribbean resorts, and so on. I suspect that, completely inadvertently, I have just opened myself up to all sorts of tempting but corrupting inducements. A few Waboba balls won't make up for the villa on the Côte d'Azur that this column has cost me, but the Waboba Surf, coming soon to a store near you, looks excellent. ✶

NOVEMBER/DECEMBER 2011

BOOKS BOUGHT:
* None

BOOKS READ:
* *Charles Dickens: A Life* – Claire Tomalin

I f I were walking home down a dark alley, and I got jumped by a gang of literary hooligans who held me up against a wall and threatened me with a beating unless I told them who my favourite writer was . . . Well, I wouldn't tell them. I'd take the beating, rather than crudify my long and sophisticated relationship with great books in that way. The older I get, the less sense it makes, that kind of definitive answer, to this or any other question. But let's say the thugs then revealed that they knew where I lived, and made it clear that they were going to work over my children unless I gave them what they wanted. (This scenario probably sounds very unlikely to American readers, but you have to understand the violent passions that literature excites here in the UK. After all, we more or less invented the stuff.) First, I would do a quick head count: my seven-year-old can look after himself in most situations, and I would certainly fancy his chances against people who express any kind of interest, even a violent one, in the arts. If, however, there were simply too many of them, I would eventually, and reluctantly, cough up the name of Charles Dickens.

And yet up until a couple of weeks ago, I had never read a Dickens biography. I have read a biography of Thomas Hardy, even though I haven't looked at him since I was in my teens, when I was better able to withstand the relentless misery; I have read biographies of Dodie Smith and Richard Yates, even though much of their work is unfamiliar to me; I've read biographies of Laurie Lee and B. S. Johnson, even though I've never even opened one of their books, as far as I know. Every time, I was drawn to the biographer, rather than the subject. (The great Jonathan Coe wrote the B. S. Johnson book, for example.) Last year I devoured Sarah Bakewell's brilliant book about Montaigne, *How to Live*, even though I can hardly make it through a sentence of Montaigne's essays without falling into a deep sleep. Expecting a biography to be good simply because you have an interest in the life it describes is exactly like expecting a novel to be good simply because it's set in Italy, or during World War II, or some other place and time you have an interest in. The only Dickens biography I have ever wanted to read until now was Peter Ackroyd's, but it is over a thousand pages long and made me wonder whether I'd be better off digging into *Barnaby Rudge*, or *The Pickwick Papers*, or one of the other two or three novels I haven't yet got around to. In the end, inevitably, I read neither Ackroyd nor Rudge, a compromise I have managed to maintain effortlessly to this day.

Claire Tomalin is my favourite literary biographer; in the UK, she's everybody's favourite literary biographer. (Everybody has one, here in lit-crazy Britain.) She's a clever, thoughtful, sympathetic critic, a formidable researcher, and she has an unerring sense of the reader's appetite and attention span. A publisher once explained to me that the First Law of Biography is that they always increase in length, because the writer has to justify the need for a new one, and demonstrate that something previously undiscovered is being brought to the Churchill/Picasso/Woolf party; and you can't leave out the old stuff, the upbringing and the education and all that, because the old stuff is, you know, The Life. But Tomalin's

Charles Dickens: A Life is 417 pages long, without notes and index – a pretty thrilling length, given the importance of the man, his enormous output and his complicated personal life. Top biographer + favourite novelist + under 500 pages = dream package, or so I thought. I have never once made this complaint here, but I ended up wishing it had been longer.

I am not the best person to review it for you, however, because I have no idea how it compares to the Ackroyd, nor to the Fred Kaplan, nor to the recent Michael Slater, nor to Dickens's friend Forster's three volumes. Who flogs through more than one book about the same person, apart from Bob Dylan fans? The reviewers in the posher papers will all have read the others, but out here in the real world, I'm presuming that if you've read one Dickens biography, you won't be reading another, and it's highly unlikely that you'll ever get around to any of them.

You'd be missing out, though, if you don't read Tomalin's contribution. It is a fantastic book about a working writer, in the same way, oddly enough, that the first of Peter Guralnick's two monumental volumes about Elvis was a fantastic book about a working musician. Tomalin, like Guralnick, ignores the myth and gets up close to the daily life – the walks that Dickens needed to take in order to write, the strange Victorian intensity of his male friendships, the money worries, the pro bono work and, above all, the almost demented production of prose.

One thing is clear: Dickens wasn't thinking about posterity. In fact, I'm betting he would have said that he'd comprehensively blown his chance of a literary afterlife: he wrote too much, too quickly, to feed his family and his ego, and to please his public. He wrote *The Pickwick Papers* and *Oliver Twist* at the same time, providing 7,500-word instalments of each every month; later, he then did the same with *Oliver Twist* and *Nicholas Nickleby*. He was also editing and contributing to a magazine, and he was up to his neck in dependents. (He supported his father and mother, and he eventually had ten children, most of them unwanted. And his sons turned out to be as burdensome and feckless as his father had been.) He was nowhere near thirty years old.

As Tomalin makes clear, there was an artistic cost. *Nicholas Nickleby* has 'a rambling, unplanned plot' and an 'almost unreadable' last quarter; the plotting in *Barnaby Rudge* is 'absurd'; in *Martin Chuzzlewit* it is 'improbable and tedious'. The second half of *Dombey and Son* wastes the promise of the first with its 'feeble plotting and overwriting'. *Our Mutual Friend* is 'sometimes tedious' and 'the weakness of the plotting is a serious fault'. (I reread *Our Mutual Friend* recently, and the weakness to which Tomalin refers would have made a scriptwriter on *The Young and the Restless* blanch.) Only *David Copperfield*, *Great Expectations* and *Bleak House* receive more or less unreserved praise, although the prissy, saintly women are always a problem, and he published *Great Expectations* with a crowd-pleasing feel-good ending. If you are feeling bad because you haven't read any Dickens and don't know where to start, Tomalin reduces your reading load by a couple of million words. The books survive because there is something of great merit on almost every page – a joke, an unforgettable description, a brilliant set-piece, a character so original and yet so perfectly descriptive of human foibles that he has entered the language – and because of the ferocious energy of just about every line he wrote. Oh, and because he was loved, and is still loved, and has always been loved. Meanwhile, *Bleak House* wasn't even reviewed in the serious magazines – they didn't bother with old tosh like that.

If Dickens were writing today, some journalist somewhere would be obliged to point out that he was living the rock-star life; there's always a slightly disapproving wistfulness to this observation when it's made about Neil Gaiman or David Sedaris or one of the other authors who routinely pack out theatres on reading tours, as if it betokens something unspeakably vulgar about our modern world. And yet Dickens got there first: it's his template, and maybe the learned thing to say is that Bono is living the successful Victorian novelist's life. Gigantic tours of the USA, with huge and exhaustingly adoring crowds everywhere? Check. Income affected by illegal downloading? Absolutely – American publishers were not obliged to ask permission to publish the novels, nor to pay royalties for them, and Dickens spent a lot of time and energy trying to right this wrong, to general American indifference. Prurient press interest in the star's private life, combined with very unwise attempts on the part of the star to manage said interest? Both the *London Times* and the *New-York Tribune* published extraordinary letters from Dickens absolving himself for the failure of his marriage. Over-hasty adaptations of the work, designed to cash in on a book's success? Dickens saw stage versions of novels that he hadn't even finished. Business relationships that fractured because of the petulant, arguably greedy behaviour of the artist? Dickens fell out with publishers over advances and royalties and delivery dates with a frequency that would exhaust even the grabbiest, grubbiest contemporary agent. The glitzy international friendships? He met presidents and royalty, and he seemed to know every contemporary writer you've ever heard of. One of the most striking stories here describes Dostoyevsky calling in on Dickens at his offices in Wellington Street in Covent Garden; the Russian's consequent account of their meeting in a letter to a friend provides a profound glimpse of what we would now describe as Dickens's creative process:

> There were two people in him, he told me: one who feels as he ought to feel and one who feels the opposite. From the one who

feels the opposite I make my evil characters, from the one who feels as a man ought to feel I try to live my life. Only two people? I asked.[2]

But it was enough. Quilp and Steerforth, Uriah Heep and Madame Defarge, Fagin and Bill Sikes and scores of others . . . If these all came from Dickens's shadow side, then we must all be grateful that psychotherapy hadn't yet been invented. If it had, some well-meaning shrink would have got him to talk these extraordinary half-human creatures into nothingness.

I found myself thinking a lot about Dickens's formative years, and the failure of his parents to care for him properly. With no educational provision, he was free to wander the streets, mapping out London in his head, registering how short was the walk between the splendours of Regent Street and the poverty of Camden and Covent Garden. He went to see his father, whose chronic mismanagement of the family finances meant that he ended up in the Marshalsea debtors' prison, where Little Dorrit's family lived. And Charles's time at the blacking factory opened up a whole new world to him, a world in which children worked, and suffered. Pretty much all you have to do as a dad is earn some money, stay out of prison and make sure your kid goes to school; John Dickens struck out on all three requirements, and is therefore directly responsible for some of the greatest fiction in the English language. I'm not saying that it's a good idea to piss your money away and let your eleven-year-old wander through the mean streets of your nearest big city. But if you do take your eye off the ball, don't beat yourself up about it: the chances are that it will all turn out OK.

---

[2] There are so many things in Claire Tomalin's wonderful biography I could have chosen to write about and enthuse over. But after publication, Tomalin came to the conclusion that this letter was probably a hoax, and there may not have been a meeting between the two great men. You should still read this book, anyway.

STUFF I'VE BEEN READING

One of the things that did me no good at all in the formative years of my career was prescriptive advice from established writers, even though I craved it at the time. You know the sort of thing: 'Write a minimum of fifteen drafts', 'A good book takes five years to produce', 'Learn *Ulysses* off by heart', 'Make sure you can identify trees', 'Read your book out loud to your cat'. I cannot tell an oak from another tree, the name of which I cannot even dredge up for illustrative purposes, and yet I got by, somehow. Walk into a bookshop and you will see work by writers who produce a book every three months, writers who don't own a TV, writers with five children, writers who produce a book every twenty-five years, writers who never write sober, writers who have at least one eye on the film rights, writers who never think about money, writers who, in your opinion, can't write at all. It doesn't matter: they got the work done, and there they are, up on the shelves. They might not stay there for ever: readers, now and way off into the future, make that decision. Claire Tomalin's wonderful and definitive book is, above all, about a man who got the work done, millions of words of it, and to order, despite all the distractions and calamities. And everything else, the fame, and the money, and the giant shadow that he continues to cast over just about everyone who has written since, came from that. There's nothing else about writing worth knowing, really. ✳

INDEX

NICK HORNBY

ABOUT A BOY

'A delightful, observant, funny and good-hearted novel'
Terence Blacker, *Mail on Sunday*

'How cool was Will Freeman?'

Too cool! At thirty-six, he's as hip as a teenager. He's single, child-free, goes to
the right clubs and knows which trainers to wear. He's also found a great way to
score with women: attend single parents' groups full of available (and grateful)
mothers, all hoping to meet a Nice Guy.

Which is how Will meets Marcus, the oldest twelve-year-old on the planet.
Marcus is a bit strange: he listens to Joni Mitchell and Mozart, looks after his
mum and has never owned a pair of trainers. But Marcus latches on to Will – and
won't let go. Can Will teach Marcus how to grow up cool? And can Marcus help
Will just to grow up?

'About the awful, hilarious, embarrassing places where children and adults meet,
and Hornby has captured it with delightful precision' *Irish Times*

'It takes a writer with real talent to make this work, and Hornby has it – in
buckets' *Literary Review*

'A very entertaining and endearing read' *The Times*

NICK HORNBY

HOW TO BE GOOD

'Vintage Nick Hornby. Very funny and very clever, and packed with wit and brilliance' *Spectator*

'Pins you in your armchair and won't let go … *How To Be Good*? How to be bloody marvellous, more like' *Mail on Sunday*

**'I am in a car park in Leeds when I tell my husband
I don't want to be married to him any more …'**

London GP Katie Carr always thought she was a good person. With her husband David making a living as 'The Angriest Man in Holloway', she figured she could put up with anything. Until, that is, David meets DJ Goodnews and becomes a good person, too. A far-too-good person who starts committing crimes of charity like taking in the homeless and giving their kids' toys away. Suddenly Katie's feeling very bad about herself, and thinking that if charity begins at home, then maybe it's time to move …

'It does exactly what it says on the cover. Hornby's prose is artful and effortless, his spiky wit as razored as a number-two cut' *Independent*

'The writing is so funny, and the set-pieces so brilliant … Hornby's best book since *Fever Pitch*' Lynne Truss, *The Times*

'Hilarious, sophisticated, compulsive' *Sunday Times*

Nick Hornby

HIGH FIDELITY

'If this book was a record, we would be calling it an instant classic. Because that is what it is' *Guardian*

'It will give enormous pleasure at the same time as expanding, in a small but worthwhile way, the range of English literature' *Independent on Sunday*

Do you know your desert-island, all-time, top five most memorable split-ups?

Rob does. He keeps a list, in fact. But Laura isn't on it – even though she's just become his latest ex. He's got his life back, you see. He can do what he wants when he wants: like listen to whatever music he likes, look up the girls that *are* on his list, and generally behave as if Laura never mattered. But Rob finds he can't move on. He's stuck in a really deep groove – and it's called Laura. Soon, he's asking himself some big questions: about love, about life – and about why we choose to share ours with the people we do.

'Leaves you believing not only in the redemptive power of music but above all the redemptive power of love. Funny and wise, sweet and true' *Independent*

'A triumphant first novel. True to life, very funny, and moving' *Financial Times*

'Very funny and extremely cleverly observed' *Mail on Sunday*

'Funny and compulsive' *GQ*

NICK HORNBY

FEVER PITCH

'Tears-running-down-your-face funny … highly perceptive and honest'
Nicholas Lezard, *GQ*

'A spanking 7-0 away win of a football book … inventive, honest funny, heroic,
charming' Jim White, *Independent*

**'I fell in love with football as I was later to fall in love with women: suddenly,
inexplicably, uncritically, giving no thought to the pain or disruption it would
bring …'**

For many people watching football is mere entertainment; to some it's more like a
ritual; but to others, its highs and lows provide a narrative to life itself. For Nick
Hornby, his devotion to the game has provided one of the few constants in a life
where the meaningful things – like growing up, leaving home and forming
relationships, both parental and romantic – have rarely been as simple or as
uncomplicated as his love for Arsenal.

Brimming with wit and honesty, *Fever Pitch* catches perfectly what it really
means to be a football fan – and in doing so, what it means to be a man.

'Funny, wise and true' Roddy Doyle

NICK HORNBY

A LONG WAY DOWN

'Can I explain why I wanted to jump off the top of a tower block?'

For disgraced TV presenter Martin Sharp the answer's pretty simple: he has, in his own words, 'pissed his life away'. And on New Year's Eve, he's going to end it all … But not, as it happens, alone. Because first single-mum Maureen, then eighteen-year-old Jess and lastly American rock-god JJ turn up and crash Martin's private party. They've stolen his idea – but brought their own reasons.

Yet it's hard to jump when you've got an audience queuing impatiently behind you. A few heated words and some slices of cold pizza later and these four strangers are suddenly allies. But is their unlikely friendship a good enough reason to carry on living?

'Hornby's best novel to date, impossible to put down … how can an examination of four people's anguish be so enthralling?' Ruth Rendell, *Guardian*

NICK HORNBY

JULIET, NAKED

Annie and Duncan are a mid-thirties couple who have reached a fork in the road, realizing their shared interest in the reclusive musician Tucker Crowe (in Duncan's case, an obsession rather than an interest) is not enough to hold them together any more. When Annie hates Tucker's 'new release', a terrible demo of his most famous album, it's the last straw – Duncan cheats on her and she promptly throws him out. Via an internet discussion forum, Annie's harsh opinion reaches Tucker himself, who couldn't agree more. He and Annie start an unlikely correspondence which teaches them both something about moving on from years of wasted time.

Juliet, Naked is about the nature of creativity and obsession, and how two lonely people can gradually find each other.

'*Juliet, Naked* is Hornby's best novel to date' *Spectator*

'Ingenious, funny and moving' *Daily Mail*

'Hornby writes so well that you can almost smell the birdseed odour of badly dried clothes combined with failure that pervades Annie's house; his triumph though is to find infinite amounts of warmth and humour in this seeming world of desolation' *Sunday Telegraph*